# Steel Wheels
# and
# Rubber Tyres

## Volume Three

*A General Manager's Journey*
*Halifax*
*Wakefield*
*Leicester*
*Krefeld*

*by*

# Geoffrey Hilditch

*OBE, Ch Eng, FI Mech E, FILT, FCIT, MIRTE*

# **Venture** *publications*

The General Manager of Halifax with his wife Muriel, daughter Diane and son Christopher in April 1967. Geoffrey had borrowed a Mercedes 0302 demonstrator coach – for evaluation – and taken it with his family to the Blackpool Coach Rally. Diane remembers being delighted at the situation – a brand new coach, and all to themselves. Chris remembers they were standing in front of an Evan Evans Tours Daimler Roadliner.

# CONTENTS

## Publisher's Preface

**W**hen our good friend Geoffrey Hilditch approached Venture in late 2012 to enquire if we would be interested in publishing the final part of his memoirs, our first question was 'will it be a warts-and-all story?' It seemed, from what we knew, that our Geoffrey must have lots to tell, and that much of it would show his reasons for making unexpected changes in his career late in life and in directions perhaps not to be expected. And so, warts and all, here it is.

We believe that through the pages of this volume the reader will find much that will – or should – concern him. Geoffrey makes no secret of his unhappiness at the vast amounts of money that the newly-formed West Yorkshire PTE would need – or manage – to spend in creating a part of Mrs Castle's new empire. Some of his contemporaries claim he did not fit into her vision of 'new blood' or even 'men of vision'.

If changing from a regime where cost-effectiveness was the watchword to one where annual losses measured in millions became the norm, then Geoffrey would probably be the first to say "Tha's right lad, that's definitely not my style". If sticking to values he had grown up with became unacceptable in some places, and having to accept political correctness and the need to put right to one side when local politics took over was going to be the order of the day, then one outspoken northerner was always going to have his head above the parapet sooner or later. Usually sooner.

And yet, as we shall see, these very values which were to cost him his job with one set of employers were precisely the ones which later brought him back into that very same Manager's office in Leicester, only this time the remit was to operate efficiently, profitably, and to do the job properly with appropriate recourse to discipline when necessary.

He made no secret with his exasperation with Leyland, being but one of the many who suffered at their hands in the sixties and seventies and especially with the axing of the Daimler Fleetline, but his work with Dennis to create an alternative must rate as one of his finest achievements.

Later, in Part 4 we shall see that being part of the Drawlane team seemed like a good idea initially, but later getting out was a better one.

Our man in Whitehall must have found many eye-openers, even after all he had been through, since he was abruptly propelled through his office door in Halifax, only to hear it firmly locked behind him, thanks to the passing of an Act of Parliament.

Sadly Geoffrey passed away whilst the project was underway in Glossop, but we feel sure he would have been happy with the final result.

We know there are others who could match some of his experiences. Shall we have the opportunity to speak also to them? We would like to think so.

# *Prologue*

As the last volume of Geoffrey Hilditch's biography was published over ten years ago, it was felt that a short prologue would be helpful to summarise the events and incidents in his career, including these two books, as described by the author. There seemed no better way of doing this than by using his own words, and we are grateful to Oakwood Press for permission to use selected extracts from these two histories.

"I was born in the now long gone 1920s in the village of Disley, our house 'Ashleigh' in Red House Lane being off the main Stockport to Buxton road which ran through the village and in those days saw relatively few cars or commercial vehicles passing up and down. In the late summer of 1931 we moved to Delph, near Denshaw and then in 1939 to nearby Oldham where my parents purchased a mixed business which, in view of what was to come in September of that year, turned out to be quite advantageous. My uncle George had married one of my father's sisters and settled in Oldham and become a tram driver. I would go and see him as often as I could and he would tell me about his past experiences as both a tram and motorbus driver, and in later years enquire as to my progress in the transport industry, telling me to keep at it and he would then see me as General Manager."

"From September 1937 I travelled daily on the train to Oldham on my journeys to and from Grammar School, but thanks to the good sense of my father's younger brother, who had not only moved to Doncaster but had taken up residence in close proximity to a couple of LNER main lines, during visits I was really seeing more LNER engines than ever had been previously the case, and my notebook began to be filled with new names and numbers. It was a series of ex-Great Central engines that took my fancy, with 'Directors' and 'Atlantics' being firm favourites. I did not then realise that in not too many years I would have a much closer (too close?) association with them."

"Now, though, I was reaching the age when a decision had to be made about what I was going to do in the days to come. The war situation in this country had looked brighter after Hitler sent his legions to march into Russia and the Japanese had had their 'day of infamy' in December 1941. But there was obviously still a long way to go before hostilities came to an end, and thanks to my evening stints with buses my school attainments were not exactly all that could be desired, even if I did manage to pass the School Certificate exams. It was time to leave Hulme Grammar School and find a job, which obviously had to be in the transport industry. Consequently, I set about the task of writing letters of application in my neatest hand to all the local bus companies, both private and municipally owned, enclosing stamped addressed envelopes in the hopes of at least receiving a reply. But when they came disappointment was the order of the day. Not one of them had any openings, not even a parcels boy, for an aspiring General Manager. So it was 'Hobson's Choice' and if the buses would not have me perhaps a railway company would. I did, in later years, have a little satisfaction in indicating to local and more senior members of the Municipal Passenger Transport Association

Oldham Town Centre in the late 1940s when the Hilditch family was living in the town. Oldham Corporation Roe-bodied Leyland PD2 260 is seen in this 1948 view.

what a treasure they had missed back in 1942; I gathered that missing me then was not a matter of regret to them."

"I then wrote to the LMS and LNER and in due course started work in December as a junior clerk at Gorton works, later becoming a premium apprentice where I worked in the machine shop, erecting shop and locomotive running shed complete with footplate trips, subsequently returning to Gorton shed. The LNER was no longer in existence. We were now in the very early days of British Railways and it was very obvious that the policy of concentration was bound to occur. It was time to go and seek a more progressive career. My entry into the road transport industry was basically due to the closure of the Oldham tramway system in August 1946, although it took some time before the end result as it came to affect me became apparent. On one evening excursion to the Oldham bus garage my attention was drawn to a most unusual bus parked in the corner of the building. In the cab I noticed the maker's nameplate which read 'Seddon Diesel Vehicles, Woodstock Factory, Oldham. There had been a piece in the Oldham Evening Chronicle a short while previously saying that the firm had taken over what had been a pre-war shadow factory where aircraft parts were made, and indeed the Corporation had taken delivery of one of the first trucks to be turned out. But buses? This was a lot more interesting."

"As soon as I was home I wrote a letter to the address on the plate, and a few days later I received a reply from Mr R H Seddon. Despite knowing nothing about road vehicles I was offered a job in the Service Department to discover all I could about trucks, and when I had been there sufficient time I would be transferred to the Drawing Office for a like spell. By now my pay had been raised to £8 a week so I was living well and quite enjoying life, but we did have

During his time at Leeds Geoffrey Hilditch worked mainly with trams. Here 528, a former London Feltham car, stands next to its replacement, a new Leyland double-decker.

our moments. We received an order for some refuse trucks for Holland, which Mr Seddon said would have to negotiate 'ginnels'. Still, no problem. It was just a case of setting back the front axle of a long wheelbase chassis as per his sketch and completion would be speedily effected. At this news my chief paled and began to point out that this was not an easy conversion. Mr Seddon was having none of this. He indicated that a shipping date had already been promised and went on to mention, rather darkly, that if the vehicles did not leave the factory on time then others not named might well do so. They did, the vehicles that is, and years later, when a certain Lancashire-based concern was taking some two years to complete our bus orders, I used to think of that incident and wonder just what went wrong there".

"I had begun to buy my own monthly transport journals and in one issue one morning I saw an advert that caught my eye. Leeds City Transport was seeking a senior mechanical draughtsman at a salary of £495 per annum, which, from an economical point of view, was not a really worthwhile proposition. £8 per week at Seddon's was worth £416 and I was living at home and had virtually no travelling expenses, so a move to Leeds would see me having to take lodgings and would make me worse off. But I wanted to be the General Manager of a municipal undertaking and here was a job that would surely give me a start in that world."

I could see no future in Leeds City Transport so I wrote to Bristol, Leyland and Daimler. My chief draughtsman did not do a lot for my morale. His words were "Once someone has left they never ever come back", but he was very wrong.

"At an interview at Daimler's the Chief Car Draughtsman had told me only a few men worked on buses and he indicated that the pay for the job would be above what I was then receiving at Swinegate, and so I accepted his offer. Now I was facing a very uncertain future. I had looked for years for a municipal transport opening, had finally found one, and was now giving it up of my own free will in the hope that I could develop my career in a rubber-tyred world. The steel wheels as they then existed in Leeds held out little hope for advancement, and I was much too young to take up the appointment at Kirkstall that I had been offered."

"A change in political control at the municipal elections resulted in a tram scrapping party coming into power and thus it became obvious that in a few years there would be no trams and possibly no Kirkstall works. I had already had the experience of trying for a job elsewhere when, on replying to a question as to what I had been working on the week before, I replied, 'New trams', the Alderman concerned snorted, 'We scrapped those bloody things years ago.' (Actually it was in 1933)."

"I travelled to Coventry the day before I was due to start work at the Daimler Radford Works via an unusual route, catching the afternoon Manchester London Road to London Marylebone express from Guide Bridge for old times sake, eventually alighting from it at the Rugby Great Central station and then taking a Midland Red single-decker on to Coventry. My stay was of only 13 weeks duration, but luck was about to be on my side again for I now saw an advertisement for a Technical Assistant with Manchester City Transport. An interview took place at 55 Piccadilly, Manchester one Monday afternoon and eventually at around 5 o'clock I was taken back to Mr Neal's office and told I had been selected."

"Manchester did, of course, have another type of bus in service in this era, namely the electric-powered trolleybus, so an early task was to learn to drive these interesting vehicles so as to become fully mobile. There were only two pedals coming up through the cab floor, the left one for power and the right one for brake. One day I had a vehicle out on test. At Chester Square an Ashton trolley coming from Guide Bridge was approaching the junction. As it was in service I gave the driver priority and so began to follow him into Ashton Centre. Approaching Warrington Street the Ashton driver braked. I had to do likewise but for an instant forgot what I was driving and pressed the left hand pedal down, only it was not the clutch. It was the power pedal. My trolley took off, we went straight ahead and the poles left the overhead wires which began to vibrate somewhat alarming. The Ashton conductor too looked alarmed for he was on his rear platform as my bus shaved his."

"On Monday 3rd January 1955 I left our Oldham home at around 7.40am and made my way to the Halifax bus stop, in preparation for taking up my post as head of the engineering department there. It was more than chilly as I stood waiting at this far from delectable spot and sad to say the 7.58 would, on this of all mornings, fail to appear. All I could do was wait for the 8.58 which finally came into view only about 20 minutes behind time. This, of course, meant that, instead of reporting to my new General Manager just after nine of the clock, I was not able to knock on his door until around half past ten, when he bleakly, or so it seemed, accepted the profound excuses that I came to make on behalf of the North Western Road Car Ltd."

"Daimlers were not exactly a 'good driver's bus' and spent more of their time in the lower gears than did the other buses in the fleet. I, perhaps foolishly, advanced this argument during a visit to Patricroft when I gently suggested that at least 125bhp would be an advantage. The net result was that on return to base I found an angry General Manager waiting for me, asking who did I think I was to tell Mr Hugh Gardner himself that his engines were not big enough? Looking back after so many years I am sure there was a recipe that would have provided Halifax with a fleet of well nigh indestructible buses and we actually had the basis of such a salvation in our hands in the form of the six Daimler CD650 vehicles, numbers 81-6. But on the other hand, if you really wanted to experience 1955 problems here were one's subjects all ready and waiting. As it was, a CD650 with an improved engine, proper power-assisted steering and air brakes would have been a winner. If only."

"The advert I had seen read as follows: 'City of Plymouth Deputy Manager and Engineer. Applications should be submitted no later than 14th March 1958'. A few weeks later I started my journey to my new office at Milehouse, Plymouth, not by tram, bus, trolleybus or train as in the days of old, but by the ferry. Once the novelty had worn off I found this part of my commuting trip rather tedious and to some extent the same could be said of my new employment, because at first I had very little to do. It was quickly impressed upon me that despite my job title being Deputy General Manager and Engineer I was not to become involved with what went on in the workshops and garage. I was also told that I was not allowed to drive buses, either in or off service."

"When, in late 1959, the post of General Manager to the Great Yarmouth undertaking was advertised I decided to apply even though there would not be any salary advantage and it would mean making an expensive household removal if I was successful. Now my predecessor had been Ralph Bennett, who was moving to Bolton as General Manager, and he had made a very positive impression. From a cost per mile view repairs were just about the lowest of any municipal operator, although I had to shudder at some of the practices that were performed. For example, on the odd occasion when an engine had to be changed, the vehicle concerned was run nose-on to a substantial garage stanchion that carried the arm of a crane jib. All the preparatory work was undertaken and then another bus was run up alongside and a steel rope was secured via the jib. One end of the rope was fastened to the affected power unit, the other to the working bus. That machine was then put into reverse and so up and out came the offending piece of motive power."

"I applied for General Manager at Halifax and a few days thereafter I received a letter telling me that my name had been placed on the short list, and so would I appear for interview on Tuesday 19th August 1963, only on this occasion this was to take place in the evening. Consequently, having spent the previous night at Oldham, I drove to Sowerby Bridge and took a bus into Halifax. By chance the bus that returned me to my car was the one by which I had travelled inwards earlier in the evening. The same crew were in charge and they, by 'jungle telegraph', already knew who their new General Manager was going to be, and so offered me their congratulations. The conductor in an unguarded moment expressed the view that there were going to be interesting times ahead, as the Traffic Superintendent and I had never seen eye to eye in my earlier period with the undertaking. My arrival back in Halifax was not uplifted by the sight of ten almost new Albion Nimbus vehicles carrying Weymann 31-seat bodies. True, they had Albion 6-speed gearboxes and exhausters but that Albion engine and BMC rear axle remained."

This former Ashton-under-Lyne Karrier WL6 has been painstakingly restored from a former holiday home by Huddersfield enthusiast Geoff Lumb. His love of the local manufacturer's products was not always shared by my predecessors in the undertakings operating them.

# *Author's Introduction*

After the publication of the second part of Steel Wheels and Rubber Tyres, I came to the conclusion that I would not write a third book for two main reasons. Firstly, from a financial point of view it was hardly worth all the effort involved. Writing the manuscript was hard enough, even though I had fortunately over the years kept a personal diary and had also retained a considerable number of records and photographs, but another considerable chore, after selecting the pictures to accompany the text, was devising and writing out all the necessary captions, with the research that this often needed. Compare the time spent on these activities with income received after tax and it truly was hardly worth the effort, even though my story was well received and sales were very satisfactory. A goodly number of enthusiasts wrote to say how much they had enjoyed their read and rather surprisingly I continue to find myself replying to quite a number of letters asking for further information even in this year of 2013.

The second reason was that the last few years of my career were rather different from the earlier ones. I went from sunshine to rain as this narrative will show and I did not leave the transport industry in the way I had imagined. Life running a bus undertaking became ever more difficult as the years rolled by for various reasons, some of these being the continual fall in traffic receipts through continued and on-going recession; the ever-rising cost of labour, vehicles and materials in times of never-ending inflation; a more aggressive attitude adopted by the Trade Unions and the end effects of far too much political interference, (the only possible word), in what should have remained as straightforward transport operation.

I have no doubt that some of the difficulties that I came to encounter were of my own making, but surely not all of them were. Now after quite a long gap, at the age of 87 and still with the benefits of a long and active memory, I can set down dispassionately in print what did happen so many years ago.

To keep the number of pages and the cover price within reasonable bounds, I have only been able to cover the more important or interesting features of the years 1974 to 1996, with a little extension to some years later. Now, reader it is all over to you, and again I hope that you enjoy reading the reminiscences of what is now a retired and somewhat geriatric former Municipal Transport Manager. Ah, those were the days!

Finally, if anyone is to blame for the appearance of part three let the fault lie at the feet of all those friends who have over the years pressed me to sit at my typewriter again and then do the necessary.

# 1 – Shades of Things to Come

**W**hen I look back over my years in the bus industry, I come to the inevitable conclusion that the best political head of the Ministry of Transport – or call it what you will – was a certain Tom Frazer MP. Now you might ask 'Just what did he do that was noteworthy?' and the answer is 'Nothing', which was why in my view he was the best, for under his regime we were largely left alone to get on with the task of running buses. But alas it was all too good to last.

He was replaced as Secretary of State by the red-headed Barbara Castle, who was obviously determined to make a name for herself, and so under her supervision the first four Passenger Transport Authorities and their complementary Executives were set up, coming into existence in the Greater Manchester area on 1st November 1969. On that date the previously independent undertakings of Bolton, Bury, Rochdale, Oldham, Ashton, the SHMD Board and Stockport, along with Manchester and Salford, had been forcibly amalgamated – with no form of compensation being paid to the local councils whose property they had been. This latter point would prove very relevant as we shall see later.

There seemed to be around this time an impression in the highest circles that professional bus men with years of experience in the field were not really competent to be trusted with the running of these new monolithic organisations, and new blood was what was wanted. Consequently SELNEC PTE, which was shorthand for South East Lancashire and North East Cheshire, came to have as its first Director General Tony Harrison, the ex-Town Clerk of Bolton, whilst the heads of the finance and personnel directorates were also outside appointments. It is true that the Director of Operations, Geoffrey Harding, was from another former municipal undertaking, but his fleet at the time of his appointment was only the size of the former Ashton-under-Lyne concern with just 75 buses. However, the gentleman concerned did have the reputation of being something of an original thinker, having a great interest in hovercraft, so perhaps this was the reasoning behind his selection.

The net result of all this was that I became sad for so many of my former managerial colleagues who had lost the status they had formerly enjoyed and who, if they continued to work, found themselves as District Managers or back as engineers or traffic officers. Even the highly competent Jack Thompson who was the General Manager of the large Manchester concern failed to be given an initial seat on the PTE Board, and so it seemed for most of my confreres that the fun had gone out of the business. They were no longer able to suggest the introduction of new policies, but had to react to ones that were handed down from those above.

If this was going to be a pattern for the future elsewhere, then it was not from my point of view a very attractive one, but thank goodness at this time West Yorkshire was not to be greatly affected by the Castle woman's machinations except in one regard which from the Halifax point of view turned out to be beneficial. Mrs Castle had mesmerised the head of the British Electric Traction group into selling its various operating subsidiaries to the State. These were then

Not a good picture, but a very typical pose of Mrs Castle making her point to delegates at full throttle.

combined with the former Tilling group concerns that had been State-owned for some years and now under the 1968 Act these became part of a new National Bus Company, which was set up by that legislation.

That same legislation required those railway officers who sat on the ruling bodies of such undertakings as the Halifax Joint Committee to relinquish their seats in favour of NBC representatives, and it was a very senior figure in the new NBC, who became alternate Chairman of both the Halifax and Todmorden Joint Committees, who recommended their merger into the Calderdale JOC and who had also in 1971 inspired the Hebble merger. So now we had a distinct traffic area with some good routes and one or two other extensions seemed very possible. All we needed now was time to develop the system to ensure it became more profitable and to remove as soon as possible from the fleet those vehicles which had come to us through these mergers and so were either obsolete or non-standard. For the future, Daimler double-deckers or single-deckers were to be the order of the day for heavy local services, with Leyland Leopards with semi-automatic transmission for rural work, dual-purpose work or full luxury coaches. But alas, time was not something we were going to enjoy, although in February 1971 when all this took place we did seem to have a reasonably secure period in front of us. How wrong can you be?

The first four PTAs were set up during 1969 and, through their Executives, the PTEs, took responsibility for operations, financial and all other controls at the rate of one per month, starting with West Midlands in October. When SELNEC took over the reins in Manchester the following month, the two and a half thousand plus vehicles they inherited represented the biggest fleet outside London which had some 6,000 units at that time. Although the Executive was staffed almost entirely by professional busmen, the initial four Directors of the PTA comprised the former Town Clerk of Bolton, a brewery Finance Director and a Personnel Director from a leading mail order company with the only busman, the Director of Operations and Engineering coming from Wallasey, one of the smaller North West operators. The Secretary to the PTA had worked in the Town Clerk's departments at Bolton and Warrington. In order to show no favouritism to any of the former undertakings, a livery of sunglow orange and white was chosen as the new corporate colour scheme and it is shown here on one of the new experimental fleet, a two door Leyland National. Mr Bennett, who by this time had moved to Manchester, was to finish his career in London, becoming another victim of the politicians. The logo, a stylised letter S, came in different colours depending to which operating unit it belonged.

SELNEC purchased various experimental vehicles for evaluation, including offerings from Leyland, Daimler, Mercedes, Scania and Seddon, before going on to design its own standard double-decker built by Northern Counties and Park Royal, the former concern being owned by the PTE. Batches of that firm's reduced height version of the SELNEC Standard later entered the West Yorkshire PTE fleet.

Halifax took large numbers of forward entrance Leyland Titan models during the 1960s, mostly of the PD2 variety, as seen above on No. 43 of 1962 with a body by Weymann, but some PD3s were also taken into stock. Delays to deliveries meant that it was 1966 before the last of this type entered service. They were not of my choosing, my preferred choice being the Daimler Fleetline with Northern Counties bodywork, one which is seen below. Coincidentally, the first example of this type in the Halifax fleet also entered service in 1966.

By now the Government of the day seemed very interested in the reorganisation of local government, and statements to that end were often forthcoming, but no consensus as to the form it might take was apparent. Local Government representatives had almost as many different views on the subject as there were Councillors and Alderman, whilst those loftier individuals who occupied the House of Commons were obviously thinking along similar multi-faceted lines. Prevarication was not going to last though, and it didn't.

In late October we decided to have a few days holiday in our Devon holiday home, and it was whilst there on Thursday 4th November, that I read a summary of the newly published Local Government Bill which indicated that two new Metropolitan Counties were to be set up in West and South Yorkshire respectively and these were to be blessed with new PTAs and PTEs, which effectively meant that my job as General Manager of the two Halifax concerns would be coming to an end on 31st March 1974. The next two and a half years looked like being very traumatic, for what had occurred in Manchester for example could well be repeated in West Yorkshire, so you can be assured that I was not amused.

In the meantime though, work had to continue in the existing way, when it would be a case of watching developments as they came to unfold. We were now firmly in a twilight zone, but at the very least we could see if it might be possible to ensure that the four General Managers who would be mainly affected by what was proposed derived as much benefit as possible from the envisaged situation, and so our meetings began to take place rather more frequently than had been the case.

Truly a time for reflection.

Hebble's days came to an end in 1971 although this was one of eight Royal Tigers purchased much earlier in 1953. The reversed cream livery soon faded and the vehicles were repainted into normal bus fleet colours. Weymann built the 44-seat Hermes bodywork.

The Daimler Fleetline pictured below was one of three bought by Halifax in 1967/8 and fitted with 45-seat bodies by Willowbrook. It became number 3107 in the PTE fleet.

Of the four, Edward Deakin of Bradford soon intimated that he was not at all interested in the future of the PTE as he would be retiring from the end of March 1974. Messrs Lord of Leeds and Rostron of Huddersfield were in an advantageous situation as on vesting day both would be over 50 years of age, so if they wished they could elect for early retirement and receive an enhanced pension. But I was the baby of the quartet, and reaching but 48 at the material time could only hope like a certain Mr Micawber of Dickens fame, that something would turn up.

We therefore proposed to our provisional masters, that the Executive should have five Directors. The head, as appertained elsewhere, would be styled Director General, whilst the rest of the Board would be made up of Directors of Finance, Personnel, Operations and Engineering. These suggestions were accepted and we then went on to agree that the remaining three of us would all apply for the DG's job with the hope of cutting out as much outside opposition as possible, and then if one of us was lucky enough to obtain the top job he would then do his best to ensure the other two remaining would be appointed to the Board. Here it was further suggested that I should concentrate on becoming Director of Engineering and Development, leaving the Operations slot open to John Rostron as he had no engineering qualifications. I must say that, whilst I agreed to comply, it was not what I wanted, feeling that Operations was going to be far more interesting and after the Hebble and Todmorden mergers I felt that I had sufficient experience in mergers to play a useful role in what 1974 would bring. But a deal was a deal and so firstly I put in my application for the top job.

The Director General interviews were held in Wakefield on Wednesday 13th July 1973 and Tom Lord was duly appointed, but apparently not unanimously so. There was, it seemed, a suggestion raised that a younger man be recruited who would have a longer term interest in making sure the PTE worked properly and well, and the point was put to Tom that he could retire in 1974 if he wanted and was not so many years from his 65th birthday, so just what were his views on the matter? His reply, apparently, was to the effect that he had no intention of giving up at any time within his possible span, and was indeed looking forward to the challenge. Of the three local contenders he was thought to be in the strongest position, being the senior with the largest fleet and the highest salary, and his Chairman at Leeds had chaired the interviewing panel in his capacity of Chairman designate of the PTA. So he was, in effect, in pole position. All this is interesting in view of what was to come. On that momentous day Tom might well have been speaking with forked tongue, but if he was then he kept his secret thoughts very much to himself.

I came away from the interview in a dubious frame of mind, deciding to apply for a General Manager's position then being advertised, the undertaking concerned being well away from Halifax and in no danger at all of being swept up into a PTE. But then my luck went into free fall. My wife and I had been invited to a civic function which was to take place in a town some miles from Halifax, so to that place we journeyed on the selected Saturday afternoon. There we met up with the Mayor and Mayoress, who invited us back to the Town Hall to partake with them of the buffet lunch that was laid out in the Mayor's parlour.

Leeds City Transport No. 78, an AEC Swift with a 36ft Roe 48-seat body and a 505 engine, was new in March 1968. After acquisition by the PTE it became No. 1278. There were ten buses in the batch, re-numbered 1276 to 1285.

It was a good lunch, but as our hosts and my wife chose food from the right hand side of the table, I selected the things that appealed to me from the other end.

We duly left for home around three of the clock and on arrival there I felt most decidedly odd. My daughter was wanting to be taken for a driving lesson but I was not able to do the necessary, so my wife sat in front with Diane and I took a back seat. Eventually, later in the evening, whatever the trouble was seemed to pass away, only to return on the Monday morning. I managed to cope with the office work all that day and on the Tuesday which, as luck would have it, was Transport Committee day. But walking from the Town Hall to the bus station, where I had parked the car, proved to be impossible and I had to have one of my colleagues go for it and then drive me back to Skircoat. I went into the office on Wednesday morning feeling far from well, but within a hour I was suffering from the worst bout of food poisoning I had ever experienced, and this state of affairs lasted for the next four weeks.

In that period I received a letter to say that I had been selected for interview for the General Manager's job mentioned above, but there was no way I could have put in an appearance on Monday 25th June when I might just have been successful. On receipt of my letter of explanation as to why I had had to pull out, no less a person than the Town Clerk had phoned my wife to ask, if the interviews were to be postponed for a week or two, would I be fit to travel. But she had to say that if anything my condition had worsened over the preceding week, and she felt in consequence that my withdrawal should be taken for granted. There, as a result, was one lost opportunity.

Some days later I received another message. The interviews at Wakefield for the next two Directors' jobs were to take place on Thursday 11th July and it was imperative that I put in an appearance, otherwise my future might well be

Had things worked out differently, it could have been my name on the side of these buses in Plymouth from 1974, but I had given my word to stay at least two years with the PTE and so that was that.

The only Leyland National to be found in the WYPTE's initial fleet, No. 1301 was 37ft 6ins long, had 52 seats and was powered by a fixed head O.510 engine. Ordered by Leeds City Transport it went into service in November 1973. I was not impressed.

very problematical. In the event, after being driven to Wakefield, the members of the PTA could not have been nicer. They asked me the absolute minimum of questions, wished me a speedy recovery and told me I was now appointed Director of Engineering and Development at a salary still to be determined, but which I was assured would be more than I was currently receiving. However, the offer came with a proviso that my acceptance was conditional on my agreeing to stay for at least two years, when in view of the kindly way I had been received all I could do was to accept the stipulation. If only I could have told the future!

Tuesday 28th August was the day when I had an approach that I could never have anticipated. By this time I was well on the way to recovery, a process that I felt would be speeded up by spending some time in what was then our South Devon holiday home. That particular morning I was stretched out on a lilo in the Torbay sun when I heard the phone ring in the next house, for what could have been the first and last time. A minute or so later my neighbour put her head over the garden fence to announce that there was a phone call for me. The initial caller then proceeded to tell me what a job it had been to find me. We did not have a telephone in the house, so after ringing Halifax and ascertaining my address, the speaker had the job of going through the local directory to try to find an address that had a phone and was conveniently close to mine. Next door filled the bill nicely.

After these initial pleasantries, that first speaker was replaced by my former Plymouth General Manager, John Timpson, who proceeded to tell me he had had it in mind to speak to me for several weeks past as he had decided to retire and so posed the all important question "Would I like to succeed him at Milehouse?" What a question to ask! In the event I went over to Plymouth two days later for an exploratory chat but then had to tell those that I then met of my recent illness and how the job of Director of Engineering had been virtually handed to me subject to me accepting that two year proviso. I had given my word and I

When John Wake came from St Helens to Bradford as General Manager he ordered a fleet of MCW-bodied AEC Regent Mark V double-deckers with synchromesh gearboxes. Here a typical example stands outside the soon to be redundant former tramway depot at Duckworth Lane.

could not see in all ethics I could go back on it, but I spoke those words with a heavy heart as a return to Plymouth as General Manager would have been the realisation of an impossible dream but I had given my word that I would stay for at least two years.

And so my immediate future was going to lie within the West Yorkshire PTE. By now John Rostron had been selected to fill the position of Director of Operations and Planning, but we were not yet, at this stage, members of a Passenger Transport Executive as the necessary Order that would make the PTE a legal entity had yet to be signed by the Secretary of State, and that other essential – the size of our respective salaries – had yet to be determined.

There was, though, a lot to think about and so we continued to meet regularly at the four undertakings in turn, when the usual form was to start with coffee and look over the developing situation, have lunch and then go for a walk round the premises when various questions might be raised. This was all very enlightening, none more so than on a visit to Bradford in the late summer.

Things started off very quietly. Edward Deakin's coffee was excellent, our discussions went well, but then came the uproar. Edward, in an expansive mood, said with a smile, "I suppose you have heard that we are to have a new bus station and interchange, so would you like to see a model of what it will be like on completion?"

I said that I for one certainly would, as Halifax still had some own-account services into Bradford and it would be useful to know where that city terminal was going to be. My colleagues expressed their interest too, so Edward rang for his steward and told that worthy to have the Interchange model brought in.

A pair of AEC Reliances had entered the Halifax 'B' fleet in 1971, and No. 261 (OJX 61K) with Plaxton 43-seat body was the second of the pair. For a while they were both allocated to Millwood depot at Todmorden.

A few minutes later two staff members appeared carrying a large plywood box, fitted with two sedan chair-like handles, being told then to place the box on our now-cleared luncheon table. We, the uninformed, gathered round, whilst Edward, with the air of a magician, swept off the cover and began to describe the wonder that lay beneath it. The new and greatly reduced railway station was not a problem, then off came the overall roof of the new bus station to reveal the covered platforms that were to be fitted with doors that would automatically open as a bus drew up to a loading point, whilst the pavements on which would be passengers would wait for their buses would be electrically heated. Well perhaps so far so good.

Off then came the floor of the bus station, only it was not just a floor for it also formed the roof of a bus garage. But did one, should one, put a bus station on a garage roof? And what a garage. Basically underground it would need a lot of artificial light and ventilation too, but no worries here as Edward went on to describe the intended contents of the plant room. Only room was not an accurate description; hallowed hall would have been a lot nearer the mark. There was though another item to be considered. This garage was going to have a signalling system to control the movements within. This was construction on a vast scale and then some.

Our prospective Director General turned red and asked who was going to pay for all this, when Edward gaily said he presumed it would come to rest at the door of the PTE, but no matter. He quickly turned his attention to the new multi-storey office block, adding that it was to be given two extra floors to provide accommodation for the Headquarters of the PTE. At this stage Tom Lord began to exhibit all the signs of concentrated apoplexy. It was a memorable scene but Edward, who would not be around when this monolith came into being, was quite unmoved by Tom's outburst and gently mentioned the anticipated cost involved. By this time Tom looked as if his apoplexy was going to be compounded by a heart attack.

Our Bradford meeting came to an abrupt end with an offer by a smiling Edward to go and look at the site being rejected out of hand. I returned to Halifax to consider what I had seen and heard, but this was far from the end of the story as future reading will show. There was a sequel to this later when Bradford was visited by members of both the PTA and the PTE. Needless to say the model was given another airing, only this time it was another chief officer of the Bradford Authority who had the task of describing its numerous features. We, the outsiders, were then invited to ask questions, so I decided to try my luck and gently enquired how this was going to be paid for. Was it to be paid for by Bradford City Transport, or was it a demonstration project when the tab would be picked up by the city rate fund, or would some combination apply? It did seem that our demonstrator was going to give a reply, but he was stopped in his tracks by a senior member of the Bradford council who told him he must not answer. Then, turning to me, the same gentleman said that as an officer I had no right to put such a question. On hearing this Councillor Harold Sheldon, who

Brief Encounter – At the first ever PTE bound Chief Engineer's meeting at Skircoat Road to discuss specifications, I had my future colleagues bring one of their latest double-deckers with them. Here are the four participants standing in the Halifax depot yard.

was the Vice-Chairman of the PTA, said that if Mr Hilditch had no right to pose the question he certainly had, so just what was the answer? Our Vice-Chairman was unlucky though as no form of enlightenment was forthcoming when Tom Lord, who was sitting next to me, muttered some unprintable comments on the Interchange and all its works. It was though all too obvious that if the Bradford Transport Department should find the Interchange costs in its accounts, then red ink must surely be the order of the day.

From the time of my appointment as Director of Engineering and Development designate I found myself spending ever less time at Skircoat Road, making almost daily trips to Leeds where I had temporary quarters in a room once occupied by a certain AB Findlay; the room in which the interview took place that saw me being taken on the staff of the then Leeds City Transport Department. With a little degree of satisfaction I could contemplate how my career had developed since what was then a long time ago in October 1950.

Eventually, the Secretary of State signed the order which brought the PTE into existence, and so we came to hold the first official meeting of the new but yet-to-be completed Board in Tom Lord's Swinegate office on Wednesday 15th August 1973. By then the three of us had outlined our thoughts as to the sort of organisation that would be needed to cement the four previous undertakings into something resembling a homogenous whole, and so we could begin to appoint staff to posts that would be contained within the proposed establishment.

From the point of view of the existing Board we would need a competent Secretary/Solicitor and that was an appointment we had full authority to make whilst Tom Lord, in his capacity of Director General, had to become involved with the members of the PTA in the selection of those who were intended to fill the vacant Board positions of Directors of Finance and Personnel respectively. In such manner did we come to the end of what I might, with tongue in cheek, describe as the phoney war. Now the battle could commence in earnest. But headquarters meant having a headquarters staff and that had to be housed in suitable premises from both a location and size point of view. So we began to spend a great deal of time as property viewers and potential purchasers. Edward Deakin's extra two floors were beginning to seem superfluous already.

The Leeds fleet contributed a number of conventional front-engined rear-entrance double-deckers of Daimler, AEC and Leyland manufacture to the new West Yorkshire PTE fleet, and an AEC Regent with locally built Roe bodywork passes the Wellington Street coach station. North Western's vehicle in the background will be leaving for Liverpool on the cross-Pennine service.

Bradford's favoured body supplier immediately prior to the formation of the PTE was Alexander, and a substantial fleet of Daimler Fleetlines carrying their bodywork were delivered between 1968 and 1972, coinciding with the replacement of Britain's last trolleybus system. There were, of course, plenty of Atlanteans too, and this one was built by MCW in 1967 but with what look like Alexander screens in the front upper deck windows. The engine shrouds were later removed.

The standard Halifax double-decker from 1968 to 1974 was the Daimler Fleetline with Northern Counties body, seen here behind one of the AEC Regent Vs with Weymann forward-entrance bodywork; both types passed to the PTE.

The fleet from Huddersfield had also standardised on Daimler Fleetlines immediately before the PTE was established, but passing through the town centre is a Daimler CVG6LX with East Lancs body with a paint style influenced by the trolleybuses which had been operated until 1968.

# 2 – Setting up Shop

Our first task, therefore, was to find a new home for the Head Office organisation that must come to be set up. There was here the unspoken view - to me at least - that those headquarters should be located close to County Hall, and as that building was located in Wakefield, the assumption followed quite naturally that is where 'home' would be. As a result, the three of us (Tom Lord, John Rostron and I), spent some of our time looking at various buildings in the area that were vacant, or about to become so. Some of these were far from suitable whilst one at least bordered on the glamorous, but in the end choice came to rest on a building that was nearly complete, and which represented a speculative endeavour on the part of the building firm responsible for its erection.

Needless to say the interior had to be partitioned off in a way that would suit the PTE when it came into full possession, so my colleagues were consulted as to just what they wanted. It was agreed that the Directors, their secretaries and the PTE Secretary/Solicitor should be located on the top floor, and so into that part of the building I moved in almost solitary splendour. On Monday 19th April 1974, I proceeded to the best of my ability slowly but surely to move the builders

The Swinegate Office of Leeds City Transport in tramway days. In earlier times the Department's offices were in City Square but by around 1912 they were regarded as inadequate. The Swinegate building followed. Costing some £32,000 it was occupied from January 1916. After its closure it was converted into a rather upmarket Hotel and continued as such in 2011.

The Bradford Interchange head office block signed 'To Let' in July 2011. The addition of the two upper floors "to house the PTE Headquarters" as Edward Deakin put it caused Director General Designate Tom Lord to blow a fuse when so enlightened. A truly memorable event!

downwards from floor to floor until they were finally pushed out through the front door, and we had a headquarters all ready to be filled with staff.

I say here almost solitary splendour because I was joined in the premises by my new secretary, but I had begun to wonder if I ever would fill that position. My excellent Halifax secretary was invited to join me in Wakefield, but came to the conclusion that with my departure from Skircoat, came the opportunity to realise certain family ambitions, so to my regret she declined, as did my number two. The next girl made a start, only to leave after a few days, having failed to reveal earlier that she had some domestic commitments that would prevent her from meeting the normal starting time, and might well give rise to further unreliability.

I then heard that our personnel department had arranged to interview a selection of would-be shorthand typists, so I invited myself to the event and told the organiser that if I saw an applicant that I thought would fill the bill then first choice was mine. Consequently one young lady's face dropped when she was told that she was not going to be taken on for the job that she had applied for, but instead would be recruited as a Director's Secretary on a much more attractive salary. She proved to be a most excellent choice, and was very helpful to me over the two years of our association.

Metro House Wakefield, which became the PTE Head Offices, is very different from what it was in PTE days. Then there was a flat front and no prominent reception area as now. All the windows have been changed and a chamferred upper floor has been placed on what originally was a flat roof.

George House, another speculative building next door to Metro House, was acquired by the PTE to house its increasing number of administrative and clerical personnel, after I had left Wakefield for Leicester, so I was never aware as to departments located there.

By this time, however, the process of staffing was taking place, and for me that fell into two parts. Firstly, there was the selection of those persons who needed to be chosen by the Directors as such, and then those who would be contained within the engineering directorate.

Our first group appointment caused the three of us surprise, and let it be said very discreetly some self-satisfaction. Thanks to the local Government re-organisation then afoot, things were not what they had been. Take the new Metropolitan Borough of Calderdale for example, into that went –

The County Borough of Halifax.
The Borough of Brighouse.
The Borough of Todmorden.
The Urban District of Elland.
The Urban District of Hebdenroyd.
The Urban District of Ripponden.
The Urban District of Sowerby Bridge.
The Urban District of Queensbury & Shelf.
The Rural District Council of Hepton.

This meant that various former Town and District Council Clerks were looking for new jobs if they did not want to take early retirement, so the three of us found ourselves interviewing various gentlemen who had previously held offices of this kind, and that was certainly a new experience. In the event we unanimously voted for an Assistant Town Clerk within the former Halifax authority, and here was another choice that could hardly have been bettered.

From a directorate point of view I knew that there was disquiet in the ranks, for this was an unsettling period, as it had been for me earlier when I wondered just what my future was going to be. Thus, I determined that as we had lots of engineering talent within the existing four now merged undertakings, existing officers would be given preference over any outside incursions, and so it came to pass. I should say too that no 'empire building' was involved.

We would have a Chief Engineer who would be my second in command, and he was the former Leeds Chief Engineer (James Pearson); under him would be three Senior Engineers covering workshops, services and development. The main workshops at Kirkstall (Leeds) and Thornbury (Bradford), plus a fledgling unit at Great Northern Street (Huddersfield), would be under direct directorate control. Each workshop would have a Works Superintendent and we would also have a Production Engineer based at Bradford where accommodation was available, responsible for co-ordinating activities in those premises and ensure satisfactory output.

The Services Engineer would cover all building maintenance and here was a cross to bear in the repair of the all-too-many bus shelters that were heading in our direction, plus the construction of new ones. A fairly small maintenance section would be set up to undertake these activities.

The Development Engineer would have Technical Assistants or Engineering Assistants located in the various constituents under him, and would also control the drawing office. This was much smaller than it had been in my Leeds days, thanks to the disappearance of the tramways and the work they provided. The former Chief Draughtsman, Harry Lister, continued in office and caused me some surprise when he began to address me as 'Sir', which indicated just how our roles had reversed, although in those earlier days he never tried to impose any authority on me. He was the sole survivor from that interesting period; the rest of the staff were new to me.

The rest of the Technical Department came to contain, besides the Development Engineer, a Senior Technical Assistant, three juniors from the mechanical side of the business, and – a new note here – a fourth who had been brought up in a body building/repairing capacity, who would hopefully bring a new dimension to this important part of bus maintenance. Again, these posts were all filled from internal existing staff.

During this period John Rostron had been building up the operations directorate, electing to have a two stream establishment at headquarters. There would be an Operations Manager and a Planning Manager, both with the necessary associated staff. In the field there would be four District Managers, one for each of the former undertakings. In every case the persons appointed to these posts were from the operations side, being existing or former Traffic Superintendents. Engineering was not favoured in these regards, but district engineering, whilst coming under the District Manager for pay and rations as it were, would also come under the overall scrutiny of the engineering directorate. They would also have technical and service section liaisons associations.

Whilst all this was going on, Tom Lord was involved with the members of the PTA in interviewing and then appointing the two individuals who would come to occupy the posts of Directors of Finance and Personnel. The chosen two were John Clarkson from the SELNEC PTE and Robin Ward previously with London Transport. Their two principal assistants were both ex-Leeds staff members; Denis Williams as Finance Manager, who sadly was not to have a long life and Eric Moorhouse as Personnel Manager who will be mentioned further in this narrative.

At this stage we were finally informed as to what our new salaries were to be, information that was a pretty long time in coming, but when it did it left me feeling somewhat liverish. As Director General, Tom Lord was to have a starting salary of £12,065 which could rise to £12,695, by three annual increments of £210. The Directors of Finance and Operations were to have a £9,366 start that could rise to £10,116 by three annual lifts of £250. In my engineering role I was to have an initial start of £9,041, which could eventually reach £9,581 via three increments of £180. It seemed to me that someone somewhere was missing the whole point; unless there are buses, there can never be a bus undertaking with finance and operations departments. It is the engineers who design, produce and maintain the vehicles, so it is the engineers who represent the foundation stone of the whole enterprise, and who accordingly should receive at least the same remuneration as their associated colleagues.

That left the Personnel Director who was to commence on £8,145, and also advance by three increments of £180 to a maximum of £8,685. I should mention here that the management of what came to be known as 'Human Resources', was the in thing at this period, but having an old fashioned outlook I really did wonder if this new department and establishment was really necessary. For example, the Halifax undertaking had managed very nicely over the years without a personnel section, but now it was to have a suitably titled District Officer who in turn would be provided with an office, a secretary and some support staff. All of this was going to entail some expense, expense that would affect the final line of the accounts. Still, we were about to enter a brand new age, so I decided to keep my thoughts to myself, sit back and see what the end result proved to be.

To continue with the salary theme, the District Managers at Kirklees, formerly known as Huddersfield, and Calderdale, started on £4,293, the local Bradford supremo £5,361, and the Leeds local chief £7,440, which was quite understandably the highest. When Tom Lord was appointed to that position in February 1961 his salary had been £3,315 rising to £4,055. The theme of paying engineers lower salaries continued at the next level; for example, whilst the Kirklees and Calderdale District Traffic Superintendents started on salaries of £3,390, their engineering counterparts received £3,165. This was something I again tended to resent, and I tried to level the playing field, but sad to say my efforts did not bear any favourable outcome. It was all rather disappointing.

Now, despite the fact that I do have copious notes and diaries written by me, it is not easy, as there are so many facets to the setting up of the PTE to take into account, to set down what I want to say in strict chronological order; so at this stage you will have to excuse me if I go back to that momentous day, namely the 1st April 1974. However, there is one more significant fact that I really ought to mention here.

By late 1974, we had attended several meetings with the members of the PTA in its designate and confirmed situations, and it was very obvious that several of the persons forming that body were employed by British Rail, and were members of associated trade unions, and, if it proved possible, were going to ensure that railways - or such that were left after Beeching's activities - would play as important a role as possible in the West Yorkshire transportation scene. We new directors were basically ignorant as to the existence of the so called 'Cooper Brothers Formula', and all that it could mean when it came to paying for rail improvements. It would become vitally important as a certain Doctor Beeching began the task of decimating much of Britain's railway network.

Finally, all that has been set down to this point really covers almost minor skirmishing, hence the title of the next chapter namely 'Let Battle Commence'.

One of a large order for Leyland Atlanteans with Roe bodies delivered to Leeds in 1970/1, former Leeds No. 412 retained its fleet number as a PTE vehicle. As the PTE's Director of Engineering I was not in favour of this sort of large window body. I wanted a more robust framing and single front doorway.

Ex-Huddersfield Fleetline 4163 passes Greenfield Station en route to Oldham. This was one of the 18 buses ordered by the Corporation that were built by Leyland with Leyland-assembled gearboxes, internal modifications that were, to say the least, very unfortunate. All 18 needed a full rebuild to Coventry standards.

# 3 – Let Battle Commence

The morning of Monday 1st April 1974 dawned bright and fair when instead of walking the few yards from my home to my Skircoat Road office, I went to the garage, took out the Jaguar and proceeded to drive to an hotel in Garforth on the far side of Leeds, there to join my two other appointed Director colleagues for an initial press conference on the benefits that should flow in the future from West Yorkshire's new county-wide transport organization. Only, of course, county-wide it was not, as the former National Bus subsidiary concerns were to continue in isolation, and here in part the PTE had lost out, thanks to the sale some time previously of Keighley Council's share in Keighley Joint Services. The running of buses in that town was now to be an entirely National Bus Company or West Yorkshire Road Car Company affair, but it is pertinent at this stage to outline the Keighley Transport saga.

On Wednesday 8th May 1889 a horse tramway was opened linking Ingrow, where the depot and stables were situated, with the Town Centre, this being extended across the town to Utley on 18th December 1889. The line, some 2.5 miles long, was worked by the Keighley Tramways Company with a maximum fleet of seven trams and, despite being almost level from end to end, which eased the lot of the horses, it never made a profit.

The service continued to run until 21st September 1901 when the Corporation purchased it with a view to converting the system to electric operation. The last horse trams ran on the night of 28th May 1904, electric traction being introduced on 12th October. A fleet of eight double-deck open-top four-wheel cars was put into service and these were housed at the 'updated' Ingrow depot. The gauge of 4ft was chosen to allow through running to other proposed local tramways, and with this laudable intention in mind a third route was opened to Stockbridge on the road to Bingley and Bradford on 10th February 1905.

The extended service needed more cars, so two more, numbers 9 and 10 to the original design, were purchased from the Brush Company, a further two numbered 11 and 12 following some time later. This latter pair was fitted with covered top decks but with open vestibules. The system now settled down to a useful if not over-profitable existence.

The Corporation had thoughts of widening its sphere of operation, and with this in mind started to run a motor bus service to Bingley in August 1909, but sadly the buses and the roads on which they ran were not compatible, and so operations came to an end early in 1915 by which time the fleet comprised eight buses. However, the Corporation still nursed expansionist ideas and so decided to invest in a trolleybus system which could act as a feeder to the tramways. But here it made a very poor choice, electing to invest in the Cedes-Stoll system which certainly was not the most reliable. This state of affairs was exacerbated by the originating company being of Austrian origin.

The Keighley operation commenced on 3rd May 1913 but in August 1914 the First World War broke out, placing Austria on the enemy side, with the result that Keighley was cut off from supplies of spare parts and was unable to progress warranty claims. It is not possible to tell the full history of this unfortunate

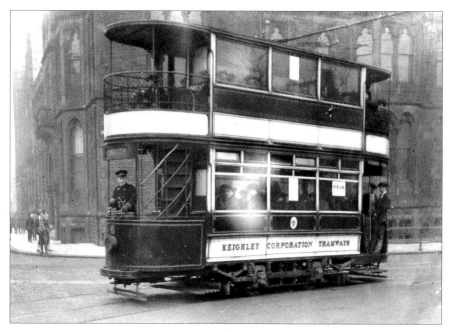

Keighley Corporation tram 6, one of the original cars dating from 1904, seen in the town centre about 1930.

One of the ungainly Cedes-Stoll trolleybuses introduced in 1913. Dodson-bodied WY 243 is pictured when new.

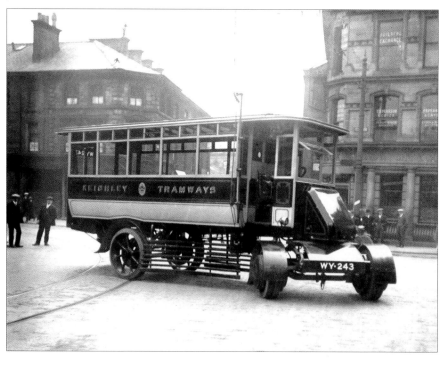

Leyland double-decker 9 (CY 1949) dating from 1923, stands in a wet town centre waiting to depart with a full complement of passengers.

This ECW-bodied Leyland Cub was delivered in March 1933 to the jointly-owned company.

system here, but the eventual fleet of nine vehicles including one unique open-topped double-decker managed to provide some service, if often of a spasmodic nature, until 3rd May 1926. In the meantime petrol-engined buses had been re-introduced from 3rd December 1921 and at this stage there seemed to be a chance that the two mile gap from Stockbridge to the later Bradford tram terminus at Crossflats might be bridged, but this was never to become a reality and here was the Achilles Heel of the system.

Two factors now loomed large. The tramway track in Keighley was rapidly wearing out, and private bus competition was ever increasing. Consequently, Keighley adopted its second trolleybus installation with eight single-deckers and ten double-deckers of impressive appearance mounted on solid tyres which began to work the tramway routes from the 20th August 1924. The last tram ran on 13th December. Under a new manager, Ronald Fearnley, later General Manager at Coventry, Keighley's buses began to improve with Leyland Lion and Lioness single deck and Titan TD1 double deck chassis making an appearance. But it was sadly all too late.

The formation of the West Yorkshire Road Car Company on 1st January 1928 intensified competition and the end was now near. On 31st August 1932 the trolleybus system was closed, and on 2nd September the Keighley West Yorkshire Joint Undertaking was registered resulting in the very last KCT bus running on 30th September after which all local operations became the responsibility of the Joint Committee. This continued to operate seemingly successfully until news of the setting up of the forthcoming West Yorkshire PTE became apparent. The Keighley Authority realised that if nothing was done the PTE would take over its assets that were invested in the JOC and so it sold them to the NBC and pocketed the proceeds. Thereafter,, if the new PTE wished to become involved in Keighley local bus affairs it had to do so via the Metro National Agreement that certainly protected the interests of the National Bus Company. However, we must now return to the ongoing PTE story.

My two colleagues were, as we have seen, Thomas Lord, formerly General Manager of Leeds City Transport, and John Rostron, who had held a similar office with the Huddersfield Authority and where, unlike Halifax, the Council had previously purchased the NBC share in the former Huddersfield Joint Omnibus Committee. As a result of that transaction Huddersfield vehicles no longer participated in the Halifax to Sheffield services and also ceased to work on the previously joint service with the Yorkshire Woollen District concern on the Huddersfield, Mirfield and Dewsbury Service.

In due course the conference came to an end, during which time I had prudently kept a few thoughts to myself, because I could not help wondering what the end result would be. I should add here that when the first PTEs were being contemplated, prior to the passing of the 1968 Transport Act, Mrs Barbara Castle, the then Secretary of State, had turned her attention to the West Yorkshire area, and had considered bringing this within the scope of the intended legislation. She had, however, been persuaded that there was no distinct conurbation in West Yorkshire as there was, for example, around the City of Manchester, and she finally came to accept that such was indeed the case. So Halifax, my former municipal undertaking, had been left to become involved in the mergers and takeovers previously described in part two of this story.

Now, however, we had been overtaken by a completely different piece of legislation, to whit a comprehensive reform of Local Government, but from a transport point of view what had changed in the intervening six years? The answer was, of course, nothing. But we were charged to do a certain job, and the sooner I got on with it the better, so once I no longer needed to concentrate on such matters as helping to locate and purchase our new offices, drawing up the engineering establishment, and sorting out which member of the existing staff would be most suitable for which post, I was able to go out on 'safari' and review my inheritance. This consisted on 1st April 1974 of 1,482 stage carriage vehicles plus a highly mixed bag of cars, vans, lorries, etc.

The buses were allocated as follows –

| | |
|---|---|
| Leeds | 708 |
| Bradford | 327 |
| Kirklees | 219 |
| Calderdale | 228 |

Needless to say the majority were double-deckers of Leyland, AEC or Daimler manufacture, but there were quite a few oddities, Leeds, for example, running a few Mercedes minibuses.

In 1970 Leeds City Transport purchased six Mercedes 406D 13-seat minibuses with Deansgate bodies. Entering service in November all passed to the WYPTE to be withdrawn in 1974 or 1976. They carried fleet numbers 30 to 35 inclusive.

This former Leeds Corporation Roe-bodied Daimler Fleetline dating from 1972 is pictured soon after receiving its new PTE Verona green livery, although it still retains its Leeds fleet number 213. This view illustrates my concern that the large expanse could weaken the frame.

The Kirklees fleet was neatly housed in two locations, namely at Great Northern Street, and Longroyd Bridge. Both were former tram depots, but the latter had been extensively modernised around 1938 to better accommodate the growing fleet of trolleybuses when the stabling lines had been turned through 90°, something I had actually witnessed in that pre-war era. Major overhaul work was carried out at Great Northern Street in what appeared to be perfectly acceptable premises whilst the much later bus garage that fronted Leeds Road was in apparent good order.

Calderdale had three establishments, namely Skircoat Road and very close by Elmwood, plus the Todmorden establishment that was held by virtue of a very dubious lease from the then Gas Board because the Municipality had failed to appropriate it for transport purposes when its small gas production facility was nationalised. I had been moving slowly to turning Elmwood into the workshops and using Skircoat solely for stabling purposes, but whilst some work had been done, paying for the infamous 'Busman's £1.00' had put paid to further short term development. The bays in Skircoat, though, designed to accommodate 3ft 6in gauge tramcars, were too restricted for comfort. Finance to provide for complete rebuilding was never going to be forthcoming though in the post 1971/74 foreseeable future.

The Bradford situation bordered on the dire, but that nettle had been grasped though was it a good idea to build a bus station on a depot roof? Time would tell and it did too. The principal bus garage that had never housed trams was at Ludlam Street, and this appeared capable of doing all that it had to as did the Thornbury running shed, whilst the adjacent works were light, airy and quite extensive but the situation at some of the other former tram sheds was atrocious. Manchester Road was on two very inconvenient levels, Duckworth Lane could only be described as totally outdated, Bowling was a virtual ruin, but a ruin that stood in what appeared to be quite extensive grounds. Finally, Horton Bank Top was something to behold. Of corrugated iron construction the whole structure was anchored by some strategically placed cables that must have been the only things that prevented it being lifted from it's totally exposed position by some of the local high winds which, but for these restraints, would have deposited the whole lot into Bradford City Square, or worse into Halifax via Queensbury. It must though be said that despite the air conditioning breezes that blew through it, Bank Top maintenance was good whilst despite the handicaps provided by their own antediluvian premises most of the others maintained acceptable standards.

This left Leeds as the only one of the four districts that had in pre-Bradford Interchange days spent any money on the provision of new garage premises. Since my days with the City Transport some of the old tramway sheds had been closed and sold off, and brand new garages had been built at Middleton and Seacroft, with Bramley being largely rebuilt and modernised. Headingley and Torre Road remained, as did the Sovereign Street 'hanger', whilst the former bus overhaul workshops at Donisthorpe Street had also been closed and its former workload had transferred to an updated Kirkstall Road ex-tramway establishment where once car number 600 had risen from that pile of apparent junk, and where Ted, the son of my former body shop foreman friend and guru Jonas Kay, now occupied the position of Works Superintendent. Leeds City Transport had outstanding orders for 121 vehicles comprising 80 Roe-bodied Atlanteans, one Seddon midibus and 40 newly-designed Metropolitans.

This leads me on to mention that Bernard Brown, the former Bradford Chief Engineer, had been promoted to fill the Development Engineer's situation whilst Harold Grundy, once in charge of Hebble engineering and more recently occupying a similar position with Huddersfield Transport, had become our Production Engineer.

Doing the rounds of this catalogue of premises, and taking in all that could then be observed, was not something that could be done in the scope of a standard working day, but it was necessary to introduce myself to those in authority in these places and to find out what they thought, and what their principal problems were when shortages of spare parts was a topic of conversation current with them all. It was, of course, a problem that Jim Pearson and I had also to try to alleviate but my in tray also bore its share of other delights so let us examine a few of these.

Calderdale had an outstanding order for another batch of Fleetlines which were intended to carry Northern Counties reduced height bodywork to meet the Todmorden garage roof problem, but Leyland delivery being what it was, six chassis waiting for Roe bodies that were then stood at Crossgates were purloined and dispatched to Wigan, a circumstance that did not please our Roe friends but

Former Leeds Daimler Fleetline No. 136, with a Gardner 6LX engine and Roe metal-framed 75-seat body, new in September 1967, is pictured after conversion for OMO service. Note the tram tracks in the foreground, a link with my first job at Leeds at Kirkstall works.

it was by then a Leyland group company and it was Leyland that was letting the side down, and Roe had no reduced height design available.

There was, though, perhaps a bonus here, for if we did not have them they could not be the cause of any actual physical problems which was not the case in Kirklees. Huddersfield had ordered a further batch of 18 Fleetlines numbered from 4151 to 4168, but these had been built at Leyland, chassis production at the model's spiritual home of Radford Works, Coventry having been closed, ostensibly to allow more luxury Jaguar cars to be built. Now, as every constituent of the new PTE had Fleetlines happily working, what was wrong with that delivery? Well quite a lot as it transpired. The Leyland people who obviously thought that they knew best had altered the form of grooving machined into the gearbox epicyclic gear drums. The result? Once only a little band wear had taken place the bands would not hold the drums stationary and slipping in gear resulted. There was only one thing to do which was to lift the boxes from the chassis, strip them right down and rebuild them with Daimler designed-components, all at Leyland's expense, of course.

This, though, was not the end of the story. The Fleetlines did have an Achilles Heel in the shape of the flexible trailing link coupling between the Gardner engine and the Daimler gearbox. They needed frequent monitoring to ensure they were in a satisfactory condition, for, if and when they came to fail, expensive damage

Eight Daimler Fleetlines were ordered by Halifax in 1972/3 with two more in 1973/4. The reduced height 74-seat bodies by Northern Counties were specified because of the Todmorden Depot access problem. As a result of Leyland's failures they were delivered to the PTE in two batches, 7001-5 in 1976 and 7006-10 in 1977, and so escaped the Huddersfield 1974 gearbox problem. Number 7003 stands in the now demolished Crossfield Bus Station.

to the drive chain could - and oft times did - result. They also needed regular changing, but provided they were subject to regular checking one could live with the problem. This batch of buses, though, began to experience all–too-early failures, so I took myself off to Leyland and went for a walk down the assembly line to make an interesting discovery. At Coventry, engines and gearboxes were properly aligned on assembly but the Leyland erectors knew not of this and so assumed that chassis construction ensured everything was automatically as it should be. Consequently, some more rectification work was called for.

Huddersfield District, or Kirklees to give it its new name at this time, had two more Seddon Pennine RU vehicles on order to add to the 21 already in the fleet, and these had also had their share of problems, both body- and chassis-wise. The body trouble was due to the absence of a body underframe, with the result that, thanks to the resultant reduction in frame strength, the body tended to fracture in the middle. Fortunately, I had been dubious about this part of the design when I ordered three early chassis for the Halifax JOC, specifying Plaxton semi-luxury coach work, but these were of the shorter 33ft length as against the 36ft of the Kirklees machines and the remedy Seddons came to provide was not applicable to them.

The Pennine RU had a rear-mounted engine close-coupled to the gearbox where a patented flexible coupling took the drive to the rear axle. This coupling could not cope with the torque and axle movement in combination, and so suffered all-too-frequent failures. The remedy was to move the engine and gearbox as far back in the frame as possible, and provide a cardan shaft to take the drive to the axle, this shaft being about as short as was practically possible.

Other Seddon problems centred on having the electrical master switch in an exposed position where it suffered from wheel spray with the inevitable electrical problems; these included a start solenoid that required a constant supply of electricity which was too much for both the unit and the wiring springs that were only three inches wide as against the four inches that would have been preferable, and excess wear in the front axle kingpin as the vehicles had been fitted with front axles of Seddon manufacture that were initially intended for goods vehicle use. The axle beam of 4 tons loading, rather than a 6-ton design, strangely a side-mounted roller bearing was included that tended to crush and lead to heavy steering.

Needless to say the Woodstock factory management was in the process of putting these matters to rights as the Pennine RU had a very promising specification for the cost involved, but the sale of the Company to the International Harvester concern resulted in the firm withdrawing from the passenger vehicle market, which was a cause of some sadness in the industry. Thus, in the interests of tidy house-keeping, the three Halifax RUs were dispatched to Kirklees to join the rest of their brethren. Similarly, the five Bradford Leyland Panthers, with Marshall bodies, were sold out of stock as they were the only such machines in the combined fleet.

There were other vehicles in the pipeline which will be mentioned later, but the most significant order was a Leeds one for 40 more double-deckers which were to represent a leap into the dark. It can be truthfully said that in this period the reputation of the Leyland concern was not of a high order, thanks to greatly delayed deliveries, tedious spare parts shortages, and the general feeling that Leyland was in a monopoly situation and could well use its power to stifle competition and then raise prices.

It is pertinent to mention here that Chacely Humpidge, the Sheffield General Manager, had been interested in buying up to 30 London-style rear-engined Routemasters, (see opposite) only Leyland top brass apparently scotched those plans and so, without an up to-date double-decker, AEC was almost certain to vanish from the bus market which indeed it did some years later.

At this stage other plans were being hatched in the bus industry, the MCW concern linking up with the Swedish manufacturer Scania to produce firstly a single-decker with Scania running units and a Birmingham-built integral body, one of these having been tested in Halifax during the later days of my managerial existence. The two partners then went on to produce a double-decker that became known as the Metropolitan, and Tommy Lord as the then Leeds supremo, being rather fed up with the Leyland situation, ordered the 40 in an effort to stimulate competition. None, however, had come into service by 1st April 1974, but now they began to appear decked in the new PTE verona green and white livery as fleet numbers 2601-2640.

AEC's only rear-engined offering was seen as too great a challenge to the Atlantean and Fleetline models and so Leyland killed it off before it became an embarrassment to its sales force. Never mind the customers' aspirations, think of the greater corporate good. Ugh.

As an aside here, we three initial Directors had pondered as to what that livery should be when, as I pointed out, Leeds and Halifax vehicles carried the colour green and had in the main appropriate interior furnishings, so after some discussion it was agreed that green should be the main colour. Some vehicles were painted in experimental liveries and it was suggested that some form of District identity should be retained, standardised appearance. Bob Davis, who had become Operations Manager, had previously been General Manager at Doncaster where he had had his buses adorned with two parallel white lines to symbolise roads and pavements and some PTE buses now began to display these markings, but in the end the cost of applying the lines by hand saw the end of this exercise and a simplified appearance resulted. The photographs show clearly what was intended and what finally transpired; but back now to the Metropolitans.

The first one duly arrived from Birmingham, and I took it out for a drive, being more than a little surprised by the experience. It was fast, very fast; and obviously had a thirst for fuel that was going to be rather costly once we had all 40 in full use. Consequently, to the annoyance of certain members of the staff, I had each vehicle as it arrived stored in the Longroyd Bridge depot at Huddersfield. I then went into discussions with the Swedish builders and instructed our new Technical Department to engage in some detailed testing. I had already decided that all 40 would be allocated to the Bradford District to allow us to withdraw some of its AEC Regent V double-deckers that possessed none–too-brilliant MCW forward-entrance bodies, and synchromesh gearboxes that in my mind were not exactly ideal when it came to coping with Bradford area gradients.

Leeds City Transport, frustrated by Leyland production problems, ordered 40 MCW/Scania Metropolitans. Delivered between June and August 1975 after the PTE was established, they were allocated to Bradford en bloc as Nos 2601 to 2640. Two more batches of 20 and 35 were to follow. Here David Bielby has caught No 2608 at the New Delight above Boothtown on the Halifax to Bradford via Queensbury service 76, which shows clearly the steepness of the gradient on this former tram route. No wonder the Spencer mechanical track brake for tramcars originated in this town. With high fuel consumption and reliability problems they were not the management's ideal and excessive rear body corrosion was responsible for their early demise.

In 1974 MCW had a specialist maker produce models of one and two-door bodied Metropolitans. Finished in appropriate colours they were given to favoured customers and this is the one presented to me, with an 18-inch ruler laid in front of it.

In due course my assistants presented me with their report. After carefully monitored and very detailed tests it was established that, as delivered and carrying only the drivers, these vehicles would achieve less than 5mpg and that the extra cost per vehicle per annum compared to Fleetlines on the same services under the same conditions would be £7,120. We were also concerned that their top speed of 55mph as against the Fleetlines' 34mph, coupled with their rapid rate of acceleration of 0 to 20mph in 6 seconds, represented a high accident potential.

Needless to say I was in full agreement with these conclusions and exerted some more pressure on our Scania friends, the end result being that an aircraft arrived at Leeds Bradford Airport carrying several members of the Scania technical staff, and in no time at all one of the test buses was fitted with so many pipes and gauges that it might have been about to undergo major heart surgery. As we were not fluent in Swedish it was difficult to ascertain just what was happening, and why, but one very interesting result was the summation of the number of revolutions made by the crank shaft during a single trip from Halifax to Bradford or vice versa. The figure was astronomical. Several days were spent in undertaking these manufacturer's trials and in the end power output was slightly reduced and a marginal improvement in miles per gallon was obtained so there was nothing left but to take the buses out of storage and place them in service and they now became a very familiar sight in and around Bradford and Halifax. Here, though, we were only at the beginning of the story, so further Metropolitan experience had best be left to my Leicester pages. I should add here that to give buses in the combined fleet an easy way of identifying their origin I had a figure two placed before every Bradford fleet number, a three before those of Halifax, and a four in front of those from Huddersfield. Leeds buses, being in the majority, kept their original identities.

At this time certain orders which had been placed before the PTE came into being were coming into stock. These included the 18 Fleetlines for Huddersfield and 40 Atlanteans with PTE-style bodies that had been sponsored by Leeds and, numbered 6001-40 with a second series to follow numbered 6041-80. Another 110 Atlanteans were also in hand together with 140 Fleetlines. Other early PTE orders called for another 20 Metropolitans, simply because of Leyland's horrible delivery situation, and for the same reason 18 Volvo coach chassis which were to have Self Change semi-automatic gearboxes (Leyland again) and Plaxton bodies.

After my experiences with the Albion Nimbus vehicles of Great Yarmouth and Halifax I was not a supporter of purchasing lightweight buses if more substantial ones could undertake the work that the Traffic Department had in mind, but I accepted the idea of buying six small Bristol chassis that were to be fitted with ECW bodies. Then, to see what other current manufacturers could offer, orders were placed for two experimental double-deckers. The first came into stock as number 3480 being an Ailsa with a Volvo turbo-charged 6.2-litre power unit located at the front of the chassis, and this was allocated to Calderdale to see how it would fare coping with the gradients in the Halifax area.

The second machine was a rather more substantial Gardner-powered Foden with a Northern Counties body. The Lewis family, owners of that company were

A former Halifax JOC AEC Reliance with a Pennine 7ft 6in wide body, repainted in WYPTE livery. One of the few single-deckers to bear the white roads and pavements stripes inspired by Operations Manager Bob Davies, previously General Manager of Doncaster Corporation Transport.

becoming increasingly concerned about Leyland's shortcomings and dubious plans for the future, and wanted an alternative chassis supplier so that the Wigan bodybuilders would have some chance of having the essential mounting bases. A limited number of these chassis, were built and put into service by various interested operators, but then the project faded when the Foden concern was taken over when an order for 30 from a new customer was in the offing. I must say I was not over impressed by the rear-engine form of layout adopted, nor the use of an Allison gearbox, but the assembly was of a substantial nature and with some more development could have become very successful.

Around this time the Dorman concern, which years earlier had supplied petrol engines that were mounted in Halifax Karrier buses was marketing a V-8 engine which had individual heads on each of its cylinders. I would like to have tried one in another Ailsa bus, subject, of course, to installation being possible, but this project never went further than being a gleam in my eye.

Of all these batches of buses that the PTE took into stock in its early days, the Leopards with their Plaxton bodies should have been the ones to give the least trouble but, alas, this was not the case. Imagine a solid piece of steel machined

WYPTE vehicle No. 7250, the experimental 'one off' Foden Northern Counties double-decker. Seen here working on the Huddersfield to Lepton service, it needed further development but that was not to be. Only about eight chassis were built, Foden withdrawing from the passenger field at the time when Northern Counties could have secured an order for a batch of 20. A Gardner engine and Allison automatic gearbox formed the drive line package.

to resemble a four inches wide road spring, which is say four inches deep around the place where it is to be mounted on the axle. The flexibility would be just about nil but it might just have been unbreakable. Now build a spring to the same basic overall dimensions, but build it up with many leaves of thin material and it would be very flexible, and the more leaves you put in for a given maximum depth the more the achievable deflection.

Our Leopards would not stand up straight and we found that different springs with a different number of leaves were fitted in various but by no means all of the same locations. Leyland's Service Department did not seem to know the answer to this problem so I asked our Chief Engineer to take himself off to the design department at Leyland which ought to know what went where, and so come up with a solution. Jim duly did the necessary, but in the end a spring campaign change was the answer, and neither of us can recall at this stage exactly what was done, in those now long gone days.

Our Volvo coach chassis order was also not doing well. The specification called for the inclusion of Self Change semi-automatic gearboxes after I had had several drives with a Volvo coach fitted with the manufacturer's synchromesh unit, but I should have known better. The Self Change Gear Company was a Leyland group concern and by accident or design – we will leave it at that – Gothenburg came to see chassis standing all complete but with an unfortunate gap where a gearbox ought to have rested. It was the summer of 1975 before the first of these vehicles, which were fitted with Plaxton bodies, entered service in the series 1506-14 with numbers 1507/8 taking to the road on 1st August, being allocated to the Metro Hanson part of the empire.

Up to this time the Engineering Department had been having things its own way, and the new standard double-deckers were built to a length of 30ft whilst thanks to some gentle persuasion they had only one passenger door. Panoramic windows were out, bodies had a sensible number of pillars whilst interior finish was to our specification, all things intended to reduce maintenance time and costs. In the first Metropolitans an unfortunate step had been placed in the centre of the lower saloon gangway and this was replaced in the second series by a ramped floor, thus eliminating a potential passenger accident problem, but there were murmurings in the undergrowth.

The suggestion was made that we ought to have a Bus Design Committee so I gently indicated that we already had one. I was then asked who was on it and I answered that it was me. I told the spokesman that it was only right and proper that the operating department should tell us what form of destination gear was required, what provision for what sort of ticket issuing machines etc should be incorporated, and what driver protection devices ought to be included, plus anything else of a like nature that might be deemed desirable, but the rest was up to us. We had to maintain the buses and the easier we could make that task, and the more we could do to enhance reliability, the better. The idea was not mentioned again during my time in office, nor was our establishing a new series of fleet numbers for PTE-purchased vehicles ever queried.

# 4 – Settling in

At the beginning of October 1974, six months after the inception of the PTE, life had begun to settle into something approaching a routine, but treat that remark, reader, with some scepticism. Metro House was virtually fully occupied, with top brass being located on the top floor. At the City end of the corridor on the east side of the building sat our Director General in what was quite a large room. I, having been the first to occupy our new establishment, had the corresponding office at the other end of the corridor, whilst the other directors plus some of the secretaries filled the other rooms along what I was known to refer to as 'skid row'.

Across the rest of the city side of the building were to be found the Board Room and the Directors' mess. Well, Tom had been demobilised after the end of the war with the rank of Lieutenant Colonel, which was no mean achievement. Against this area lay a kitchen and servery whilst on the other face of the building were to be found the offices of the Secretary/Solicitor, his assistant and the rest of the secretaries that served those of us located on the top deck.

At ground level was an under-building car park, and also on this level was the main entrance with a reception area, the entrance to the lift, and the opening that led to the staircase, and the 52 steps that brought one to fourth floor level. On the intermediate floors were the Finance Department, with the largest Metro House staff, the Planning and Operation sections, the Engineers and last but by no means least our Personnel Department.

Now most mornings my first task was to extract the car from its Skircoat Road garage and drive the 16 miles or so to Metro House, which made quite a change and could, depending on traffic conditions, occupy anything up to an hour. Previously, I had almost been able to go from my bed to my desk without ever being in the open air, and to my mind there never was a better commuting journey. Travel meant using a car and whilst General Manager at Halifax I had always run my own, being paid a mileage allowance. The financial advice we now received was that we should run company vehicles, this being – or so it was alleged – more advantageous tax-wise, so my Jaguar was sold at book price to the PTE as were my colleagues' cars. However, complications followed as the drive from home to Metro House was regarded as pure commuting and so attracted a tax charge, whilst going say from home to Kirkstall Works was regarded as a working journey and so was free of tax.

My then Jaguar was a 420 model, but Tom had an XJ6 with a 2.8-litre engine. I took it out for a test run and was appalled by vibrations that occurred at any speed over 50 mph, something that was not eliminated until two tyres were changed and every wheel carefully balanced. Before the year was out that car had been replaced by a second hand maroon XJ6 4.2-litre with the interesting registration number PTE 333M. Our Director General was very proud of this vehicle, but later was far from pleased when he found out just what tax bill it attracted when perhaps the advice we had been given was not as good as it might have been. Fortunately, thanks to my short stay, I did not suffer such an imposition, but my other former colleagues did, and far from happy they were. I too came to be provided with a second-hand Jaguar, a green 2.8-litre model, but these smaller engines had a bad habit of virtually blowing up as mine did on the M1, so when I came to leave I left that car behind, despite a new power unit having been fitted.

But what happened on arrival at Metro House? Monday was Board Day, so a prompt arrival was necessary to give me some time with my secretary to look over the post, and perhaps to have a quick word with my deputy, Jim Pearson, who had more time to spend out in the field than I had. We would gather in the Board Room for ten of the clock, to be invariably faced with an agenda that covered up to 30 to 35 items. We began to work on these as the steward served coffee, but progress was seldom meteoric and by noon we might have cleared from eight to ten, but don't bank on it. At noon the Chairman and Vice Chairman of the PTA would appear to discuss what was occurring in the political world that would be of interest to us, and then they would stay for a working lunch when plans might be hatched, but hopefully by 2.15pm at the latest we would be back in session working our way, still slowly, down the agenda so that by say 4.00pm another ten items might well have be cleared. But then, as I will explain later, the whole tenor of the meeting began to change when extracting oneself from the Board Room could become a mite difficult.

This, though, was only one meeting. You went from one to another in very quick succession, taking in meetings with NBC representatives which could be held at our headquarters, or in the Wakefield West Riding Offices or at the London NBC headquarters. Then there was the Rail Council, the monthly meeting in County Hall with the PTA members, Trade Union consultative committee meetings, previously unplanned Directors gatherings, meetings with outside Councils or suppliers and those occasions when the District Managers met the Board.

It did seem here that April the first, 1974 had seen the dawn of a new era, and plans were in motion to improve the bus and train services to a considerable degree, but by October 1974 it was beginning to be apparent that the necessary finance might just not be forthcoming and thoughts of economy were put forth, initially in muted tones, but they did become rather more strident ere long.

Tom Lord was a most interesting character. When on form he was very good company with an astute brain, and oft times the ability to come up with rather tortuous solutions to an apparent problem. I well recall one afternoon when we were gathered in the Board Room and Tommy began to tell the District Managers that they should forthwith begin to cut the services but NOT the timetables. Our more junior colleagues looked bemused by this but did not ask any questions before they were dismissed when Tom began to expound on the poor quality of the former attendees who were now safely out of earshot. When his grumbling ceased I decided it was time to have a few words, so I indicated that as he was a powerful performer, with an oft times dominant personality, the District Managers were in consequence somewhat in awe of him, and not wishing to appear foolish in front of the Board had refrained from asking the obvious question. I for one did not understand what he meant so would he please enlighten me. Tom asked, 'If you were having a house built and wanted to stop construction what would you do?'

My answer was to stop paying the builder.

The 70 Leeds AEC Swifts in the series 1001 to 1070 should have been enthusiastic performers. At 36ft long and with Park Royal bodies they were powered by AEC 691 engines. Number 1004 bears a brighter livery than earlier Swifts. Most entered service in July 1969, the remainder by November.

In the last months of 1969 Bradford City Transport put five Leyland Panthers with Marshall 36ft long 45-seat bodies into service, which later became WYPTE numbers 2508-12 The only Panthers to be acquired by the PTE in April 1974, I had them withdrawn early as being a non-standard type, all being sold to Chesterfield CT. Photographs of them in their Bradford days are hard to come by, but my old friend Stanley King found this view for me of 2508, the first of the batch (new October 1969, NAK 508H) leaving the City Centre for St Enoch road top, a Wibsey short working.

The Halifax to Leeds service was started by Hebble. After the Halifax JOC takeover in 1971 it was worked as service No.8 on a 30 minute frequency by four buses. Renumbered 508 by the PTE it was extended in Leeds from City Square to the Central Bus Station when a fifth bus had to be added. David Bielby photographed number 7002, one of the first buses to be placed in service by the PTE, passing through Stanningly Bottoms en route to Halifax. The bus was new in1974 and was a Northern Counties-bodied Fleetline, one of five delivered from Roe, due to production delays.

'No' said Tom 'you cut off the supply of bricks. It is just the same with buses; cut off the supply. Take say 20 out of the Leeds fleet, 12 out of Bradford, and 8 out of each of Kirklees and Calderdale. Each district runs a series of peak hour journeys that do not figure in the timetables, so they would have to reduce these and so promote greater economy. Do it Geoffrey, take them out starting tomorrow!'

I inquired if this was a serious proposal, to receive the answer in the affirmative, so I promptly demurred saying that I would if the Board passed a formal minute to that effect, when I would wish the record to show that I had not spoken in support of the idea, and refrained from voting thereon. The feeling crossed my mind that here was a possible policy that would quickly be reversed, and if the buses could not be returned to traffic quickly, having, say, lost numerous parts that were then in short supply, there was no doubt as to where the blame would come to rest. As it was we passed on to talk of other things, and so one of our DG's bright ideas never was taken up.

As I have indicated, Board meetings could go on at length, but one thing we never seemed to see was an up-to-date financial statement showing a true picture of our affairs. We were, of course, spending money, and some projects were to be financed by the PTA, these being discussed when we Directors met that body in the heady atmosphere of County Hall, whilst reference was oft times made to

The twenty-strong second series of Metropolitans delivered in January and February 1976 were also allocated to Bradford. David Beilby also took this picture of 2647 picking up in the city centre while working on the Duckworth Lane service. This bus lasted until November 1982.

certain costs being allocated to a suspense account – which again never appeared in detail – but cost control did appear to be conspicuous by its absence. One Saturday afternoon in the spring I was walking in the Halifax town centre when I met Ambrose Leary who was head of the Calderdale traffic department and then asked him did the office still produce the sort of monthly statements that had been the norm during my time as General Manager, because if so I would like to see one. Ambrose confirmed that they continued to be made up, and indeed the statement covering the year to the 31st March 1975 had been completed the previous week and he would deliver a copy to the house by tea time. He was as good as his words, and I still retain that sheet, and all the ones for the 1973/4 year. It made very uncomfortable reading.

At the 31st March 1974 the Corporation services had recorded a loss of £1,161, and the Calderdale Joint Committee had also been in the red to the tune of £4,142, so add them together to produce a combined loss on the year of £5,303. These losses were due to that year's wages awards, and I had wanted to seek a fares increase from January 1974, but both Committees said 'No! Let the intended PTA/PTE do what might be necessary'. So, to be fair, the Calderdale District was loss making from day one (1st April 1974). However, now compare that to the end result on the sheet that Ambrose had given me, which showed a loss on the 1974/75 financial year of no less than £1,092,353. It was unbelievable. If this was typical of what was happening in the Districts trouble would be heading our way fast, and yet there seemed little I could do about it. Let us, though, at this point digress, and take a look at some other very pertinent features.

Labour relations will be a useful starting point, and it is not hard to realise that welding four previously independent units, each with its own tribal customs, is not going to be a simple matter and this is where our new Personnel Department was bound to be very much to the fore, as it was responsible for staff negotiations. To further this part of the business, Joint Consultative Committees were set up, the two major ones consisting of Management and those staff members covered by agreements with the Transport and General Workers Union, and the one made up of Management, and those representing the members of the skilled craft unions. I soon found myself a member of both bodies, whilst other consultative machinery covered negotiations with the Inspectors, or with those working within the various administrative sections. It seemed that by and large our Personnel Director colleague was left to get on with it and then to solve his attendant problems. Now it is more than possible that at 87 my memory is not what it was, but I cannot recall any momentous labour problem being fully discussed at a Board meeting, or when wage negotiations were in the air was any indication forthcoming as the percentage rise that might be finally offered as a maximum, plus a sight of the cost thereof that could be regarded as acceptable within official circles.

It soon became clear though that our trade union representatives had gone into an early huddle and had trawled through each and every local agreement and highlighted the best and most advantageous parts of each. These were then amalgamated into a draft document that represented the ideal, and so provided the union side negotiators with a series of suitable targets to aim for. Now, in any negotiations management is virtually bound to make some form of concession

Leyland Leopard 8523 was one of five fitted with a 43-seat Plaxton Derwent dual-purpose body, semi-automatic gearbox and an O.680 engine. Delivered in March and April 1976, all were allocated to Calderdale and 8523 is seen working the Halifax to Midgeley service.

Number 38 was one of a batch of Eastern Coach Works-bodied Bristol LH single-deckers purchased in 1974 for rural services. It was photographed below while on test at Ringstone Reservoir on the infrequent Halifax to Dean Head and hourly Elland to Ripponden routes.

but what is sauce for the goose is also sauce for the gander, so if the unions gain an advantage various goodies have come the other way to make operations that much more efficient. Sadly, the PTE did not seem to be enjoying much success in these aspects of the matter, and perchance too much was being lost or given away with no corresponding benefits coming our way.

Early one morning as I was extracting my car from its Skircoat garage two members of my former staff were passing and each bade me 'good morning'. Both were trade union representatives and the senior of the pair went on to add some extra words. 'That were a good result at yesterday's Joint Consultative meeting. We would not have got it if thee had been present.' I replied to the effect that there had been no JCC meeting the previous day, but my informant persisted and went on to add that from the next pay week the first 50p of everyone's weekly 'shorts' would be written off. Now in 1974 50 pence was worth a lot more than it is today, and when one considered how many staff members were taking in fares some simple arithmetic soon gave one an idea of the amount of revenue that could leak away in twelve months.

My journey to Wakefield was undertaken at a higher speed than normal, and as soon as I was on the top floor of Metro House I went straight into the office of John Rostron who, as it was still not 9.00am, was reading the Yorkshire Post. I remember clearly saying to him 'John, are you not the titular head of our Traffic Department?'. John lowered his spectacles and replied that such did seem to be the case. Then I asked the next question 'Whatever were you doing at yesterday's JCC?' John replied that there was no such. So I told him of the conversation I had had in Halifax some 40 minutes earlier, and what I had been told about writing off those fifty pence worth of shorts per week.

John left the office in a rush to return to mine in only a few minutes to say that it was all too true, and then he also settled down to do a spot of arithmetic. I soon began to adapt the saying that was much in vogue when we had an empire namely, the sun never sets on it', only in my version the sun never set on our labour difficulties, and these could be quite unexpected.

One afternoon I decided to pay a visit to Thornbury Works so I parked the car and walked down the avenue to the big barn-like door that represented the main access for the various vehicles that the premises had to maintain. Set in this door was a wicket gate for spasmodic staff entrance and exit, and through this I stepped to find the whole of the workers standing behind it. The net result was akin to the passage through the Red Sea as the multitude parted to let me pass when my hopefully cheery 'Good afternoons' received little or no response.

I hastened to the high level offices built against the far wall, invading Victor Midgeley, the Works Superintendent, to ask three questions. The first was what on earth was going on to which Victor replied that he did not know. The second was had he asked the Personnel Department to put in an appearance? The answer to that was in the affirmative but that they were too busy currently to come to Bradford! Question three was could he see the Works Representatives in the assembly. The answer to this was 'yes', so I told him to go and bring them to the office.

Now please believe me when I say that I now have no memory at all as to just what the problem was but such was the insignificance that within less than ten minutes every one was back at work, and after a walk round to view what was happening, I was able to make my way back to Wakefield and Metro House.

One morning not long after I had left the PTE I was having my breakfast in a London hotel when who should walk in but the Leeds area T&GW full time officer, with whom I had had dealings during my time both at Halifax and at Wakefield. He asked could he join me, and we had a most interesting and very friendly conversation during which he said that for the first time in quite a long negotiating life he had refused a management offer that ostensibly would have put more pay in his members' pockets, or would it? 'I was at Metro House the other day' he said, 'and I was offered one-man-rate whenever our chaps drove a private hire vehicle, but if I had accepted it then there would not have been any more private hire operations run by the WYPTE. It would have been priced out of the market'. I made no positive response, but I had no reason to suppose that he was telling me anything but the truth.

I would query that last figure, not knowing how it was built up, but in some ways, coping with the new PTE/PTA relationship was quite difficult. In municipal days the object of the exercise was to run a fairly small locally-based operation, and if at all possible make it pay, or at least make it break even, unless the owning local authority had decided for political reasons that it was prepared to finance at least a part if not the whole of the operation. The PTE had come into being at a time when none of the four merged undertakings was doing all that well, and there was some doubt as to just what was the final financial situation of some of the districts. It was suggested that at 31st March 1974 the Leeds undertaking had broken even, but that situation did seem decidedly suspect, and I was never to know just what the Leeds, Bradford and Huddersfield's true situation was. In his most excellent work 'Leeds Transport Volume 5 1974-1986', Mr J Soper says that at 31st March 1974 Leeds City Transport recorded a loss of £1,353,406; Bradford £714,412, Huddersfield £246,783, and Halifax/Calderdale £148, 570.

Together they show the PTE's sad inheritance. I cannot recall any report quoting the situation, or anything like it, and no early steps were taken as I recall to achieve a balance. Thus was the PTE set off on the road to acute financial problems from day one.

Now in effect the PTA would finance the network, and cover the losses made on socially desirable services and if, for example, a wage increase had raised costs then the PTA would consider just what effect a set of revised fares scales would have on the passengers and if this should be accepted in total or only in part. Here the PTA could levy a precept on the local district councils to restore the balance, and precepts could easily become very dirty words within the walls of the various local town halls. Just consider again what had been, and what was now.

It was not now a question of the Bradford City Transport Committee and the City Council deciding if the local transport undertaking should be subsidised for some reason, and if so by how much, and so dealing with what would have been a purely domestic matter. Now the PTA had to take a Metropolitan County-wide view and in so doing pay full regard to a three-faceted situation where the PTE would act in an agency capacity. Facet number one would relate to the PTE's direct operations which hopefully were to be run on as economical a basis as possible, but there was a considerable certainty in my mind very early on that this forced amalgamation had only resulted in vastly increased costs. Witness here the Halifax undertakings financial record as detailed earlier in these pages, but there should have been some compensatory savings when the PTE came into existence.

For example, again taking the Halifax undertaking, legal and secretarial services were provided by the Town Clerk's department. Wages were calculated, and much financial work undertaken by the Borough Treasurer and if any building work was required then Borough Architects or the Borough Engineer were called in to do the necessary. All these and more gave rise to the inclusion in one's transport accounts of that interesting heading 'Central Administrative Charges', but as the PTE was doing all this sort of work on an in-house basis all these previous on-costs should have disappeared for ever, 'should have' being the operative words here.

The other two facets covered the National Bus and British Rail situations. The 1968 Transport Act (given Royal Assent on 29th October 1968), which was the foundation stone of both the PTA/PTE birth and the inception of the National Bus Company (set up from 1st January 1969), required all three bodies to co-operate with each other as might be necessary within the boundaries of each PTA-designated area with a view to providing as much of an integrated transport system as was possible but the word 'integrated' seemed to have different meanings to different people. What did though become very evident very quickly was that these nationalised concerns adopted the principle of saying we will do whatever you want us to, but there will be a relevant charge on a cost plus percentage profit calculation. Some of the proposed charges too were quite breathtaking.

The suggestion was soon made by the PTE that the platforms of some of the stations on the Bradford and Leeds to Ilkley routes should be raised, but the charge for the work suggested by BR was out of this world. I suggested at the Rail Council, where we were discussing these possible improvements, that we could do the work to a very suitable standard at a very much reduced cost using direct labour, but my words were coldly received and it was made very clear that only British Rail staff could and would work on British Rail properties.

I did though gain some interesting experiences thanks to my involvement with the Rail Council. BR suggested that some new trains should be acquired for the area, at of course West Yorkshire expense, and so I was taken to Glasgow and to London to look at and ride on the new trains to be found working in those areas. During the London excursion I found myself standing on a balcony overlooking the platforms of Waterloo station at a time when numerous commuter trains were entering the station and then disgorging their loads of work bound-passengers. The loud speaker system was playing some tune or other until this was suddenly replaced by some upbeat military march when the effect on those leaving the platforms was quite remarkable. It was a convincing demonstration of how to empty a train without really trying. Another excursion was a visit to the headquarters at Derby of the Train Design department, where I was shown and was able to discuss drawings of what could be thought to be new designs that might be suitable for use in our PTE area, but I was not over-thrilled at the way in which to include as much accommodation as possible rather too many seats were lined up against quite substantial window pillars.

It was, as I have said, all very interesting but in the event no new trains came into use during my employment at Wakefield. We did though find some of the local rail services being worked by the units based on the design of the Workington-built Leyland National single-decker bus, the riding of which could only be described as atrocious – as was still indeed the case quite recently when I rode on one just before the line from Oldham to Manchester closed for Metrolink conversion – and I did not enjoy the experience.

However, let us return to the main theme of this part of my narrative, and look in greater detail at the situation appertaining to the National Bus Company and its local subsidiaries. The NBC was in pole position by virtue of its some six years of experience with the original four PTE/PTAs. We, by comparison, were but uninformed beginners.

Section 24 Sub-Section 2 of the 1968 Transport Act was the piece of legislation that called for 'co-operation between relevant parties to secure the provision of a properly integrated and efficient system of passenger road transport to serve the needs of the new Passenger Transport Authority area' and this, of course,

One of the unloved Pacers. During the last days of the heavy rail service on the Manchester to Oldham line prior to its conversion to Metrolink, Colin Reeve photographed a Shaw to Manchester Victoria train arriving at Failsworth. At the time of publication these class 142 units were still operating on quite long distance journeys out of Manchester, and were set to do so for some years to come.

being still on the Statute Book came to apply to the WYPTA area as was the case elsewhere. The four local NBC concerns, namely West Yorkshire Road Car, Yorkshire Woollen District Transport, The West Riding Automobile Company and Yorkshire Traction, being under overall common management, came together to form a local combined negotiating group.

This was then ready to take part in the ensuing proceedings. A new company – the West Yorkshire Metro Transport Management Company – was then brought into being together with a formal agreement, the task of these being to do exactly what the aforementioned piece of legislation required. On the Company Board were representatives of the PTE and the four NBC concerns, plus the NBC Regional Director, and the agreement contained the sort of clauses that one might expect.

For example each party was to be entitled to operate a minimum percentage of the total mileage that might be worked in the PTA area. The Executive should be consistent with the policies of the Authority in deciding the pattern and level of the 'in area' services and the fare levels including concessionary and special fares therein, and could request the Management Company to re-organise any necessary service/s that might come thus to be effected. The Executive could also specify the colours of the buses that were to be employed in the designated area, and also require that an adequate standard of vehicle was used.

Now came the important bit. In each accounting period the Executive had to provide the Management Company sufficient funds to enable it to pay the Companies the agreed costs incurred through the operation of the relevant services, both direct and indirect, plus the proper replacement of associated assets, assets here meaning land, buildings and vehicles etc. The Companies had to account to the Executive each four weekly period for the amount of revenue taken from passengers both picked up and set down in the designated area or who were carried on services which would take them over the boundary. Cross boundary services and services joint with NBC concerns based outside the scope of this agreement also had to be catered for.

What is set down here is only the bones of what was to be a comprehensive agreement but one final clause has to be mentioned, this giving the Executive the right to audit the claims and figures submitted to the joint Management Committee via the local companies.

Now for some of the end results. There were, for example, no direct PTE services in the Wakefield area prior to the takeover of the United Services partnership, nor were there any in and around Keighley, the NBC concerns reigning supreme. Generally speaking NBC fares were higher than those of the PTE, at least initially, something that oft times was all too clear if one booked to the last outward terminus of some ex-municipal route and then making a second trip took a ticket to the first NBC stage beyond that terminus. Consequently, now the PTA in its wisdom could direct the PTE to ensure that such charges should be subject to a gentle tapering out, or that common local fares should come to exist on all stage carriage services being provided in the area of the PTA. Obviously some 'make up monies' were going to be demanded under the terms of the Management Agreement by the NBC side which, in turn, might mean

As explained in the text, the four local NBC subsidiaries in West Yorkshire came together under the Metro agreement. Because of its antecedents, West Yorkshire Road Car tended to have a predominantly Bristol fleet. Seen here in Bradford during the time the city still operated trolleybuses is one of their Bristol VRs. After I had left Yorkshire, NBC vehicles commenced using the 'MetroBus' fleetname and some were even painted in a PTE-inspired livery. West Riding, one of whose Leyland Nationals is depicted here, had not been without its own problems, requiring large numbers of buses to be transferred into the fleet mainly as a result of the problematic Guy Wulfrunians. This particular Leyland National originated with Plymouth City Transport.

As the NBC's standard single-decker, numerous other Leyland Nationals were to be found in the West Riding fleet. Examples of the first series of the model are seen below, whilst an example of the re-engineered second series is seen above alongside a Leyland Olympian. All the vehicles carry 'MetroBus' fleetnames and the inter-linked logo depicting West Yorkshire PTE's white rose symbol together with that of the NBC.

that the PTA would have to precept the local Authorities in the Metropolitan County resulting in a levy being charged to numerous ratepayers who say living in Calderdale where fares were reasonable on the whole, would derive little or no benefit from the extra cash that they had to provide. This could become a very political business so it behoved those Officers who were going to become involved in these matters to be careful, and to ensure that they spoke only in purely transport terms.

Now, prior to 1st April 1974, the former Leeds undertaking had pioneered the introduction of a travel card which was priced at £5 and which gave one month's travel on its services. Use, however, was restricted to journeys made wholly within the boundaries of the City, but from 13th October 1974, under the auspices of the PTE, this was given the new name of 'Metro Card' and was made available for use on all services within the designated area irrespective as to whether these were worked directly by the PTE or by the NBC concerns listed above. To this list of names were added those of United and East Yorkshire whose vehicles worked on joint services into the designated area with their sister companies. You can imagine the substantial negotiations that were necessary before agreement was finally reached as to just how much money would be provided via the PTE to cover the assessed loss of revenue that would be suffered by the NBC subsidiaries from accepting these cards. Perhaps, fortunately in this regard, the top engineering member of the PTE staff did not really become involved in working out the detail, but as an Executive Director principle was a different matter. Needless to say, however, the price for purchasing one of these concessionary cards that were available for use over a very wide area did not stay at £5 for long and by the time I had come to leave West Yorkshire the price had risen to £8.50. Half fare county-wide travel for OAPs and free travel for blind persons followed just a few months later.

It is pertinent to mention here that the suggestion was raised that the NBC might care to consider selling out its county-based services, but the answer to the query was a very emphatic 'No'.

All this meant being involved in still more meetings but there was one which can only be described as being of 'concrete' form and this involved the on-going building of the infamous Bradford Interchange. These meetings took place on a very regular base and included the British Rail architects who had undertaken all the involved design work, the Quantity Surveyors who were supposed to be overseeing the construction work, and, of course, the contractors who were involved in the processes needed to ensure that in due course it could be brought into full operational use, plus our Services Engineer etc. I was able to ensure that some simplification took place, with a useful reduction in attendant costs; thus the signalling system never materialised, the idea of fitting the passenger waiting shelters with underfloor heating was forgotten and those same shelters were not fitted with sliding doors that would open automatically as a bus drew up besides them. Not, I should add, that the design of the operating mechanism had actually been brought to a satisfactory design stage. But this was a mere detail.

Another job included here was to sign the cheques to cover the builders' monthly construction certificate and so for the first time ever I signed a cheque for over one million pounds, wondering as I did so just where the money was coming from. But no matter; the cheques were honoured on every single occasion. What we did not know then or find out until later was that the waterproof membrane that was intended to stop leaks from the bus station floor penetrating the underground garage was being damaged – apparently by the boots of the workers as they trampled over it during the surface laying process. But that was all another story in which I had no involvement. The Interchange finally opened on Sunday 27th March 1977. It cost some £16,000,000 with running costs of £2,300,000 per annum.

Additionally, unlike the 1968 generation of PTEs, we continued in membership of the Municipal Association of Public Passenger Transport Operators, something that saw me elected to the position of Vice President, and allowed me to continue as a member of the Motor Bus Committee. These activities involved still more meetings, often in London or elsewhere.

Other meetings in which I played a minor part were those leading to the purchase of the businesses of certain independents who had come to the conclusion that now was the time to sell out. This process had begun locally when in 1969 Huddersfield purchased the stage carriage services worked by the well-established Hanson concern of Milnsbridge in that town. Now the Hanson Board elected to sell out the rump of the business and so, on 1st May 1974, the

The complexity of the construction of the garage roof at Bradford Interchange as originally built is clearly displayed in this photograph. Was it quite an appropriate location for the PTE to acquire? It certainly was magnificent but far from commercially viable or even desirable.

PTE acquired the then Huddersfield depot in St Johns Road, the staff including manager Gilbert Fox and 23 coaches all based on Ford chassis plus two non PSV minibuses, for a price of £297,000. With these assets came a selection of excursion and tours licences plus some long distance summer express operations.

One of these covered a Friday night outwards journey from Huddersfield to Torquay which arrived early on the Saturday mornings and returned a few hours later after the drivers had time for rest and refreshment. Having a seaside home in Torbay I used the outward run on a few evenings but soon came to the conclusion that overnight coach travel was not for me. Later in the summer we came to acquire our first PTE toilet-equipped executive coach, with servery and coffee making facility.

I allocated it one Friday to the Torquay run and during the night tried to add to the comfort of the passengers by providing them with a hot drink but sad to say our new water boiling facility failed at a fairly low temperature so there never was a drink service. I was not too overjoyed to find the Fords, although I recognised that they were cheap to buy, so before too long Metro Hanson, as the firm had now become, found Leyland and Volvo machines replacing some of the Fords.

A smaller acquisition was that of Baddeley Brothers of Holmfirth, a town now famous for its role in the BBC comedy series 'Last of the Summer Wine' and earlier of Bamforth postcard fame. This local concern, which ran excursion and tours plus a limited stage carriage network, came into the fold on 24th March 1976 contributing 14 vehicles comprising ten assorted Bedfords, one Leyland and three more Fords. This outfit was given the revised name of Metro Baddeley's from take over on 24th March 1976 after I had left the PTE, but I had wondered why we bothered for if the original company could hardly make it pay with their local operating costs, then a PTE profit on Baddeley operations could hardly be expected. In the event both concerns became heavy loss makers accounting for £400,000 by 1978. Unsurprisingly, Hansons was sold off on 1st April 1979 and Baddeleys followed on 1st January 1980.

The most interesting takeover, though, was that of United Services which was not a company as such. I had often seen blue vehicles bearing the fleet name 'United Services' during my boyhood visits to Doncaster as they came down York Road and over North Bridge, and always intended to go for a ride on one being attracted by the Dennis vehicles that seemed to be the regular performer. Now, years after, I discovered that there had once been three partners but over the years this had reduced to two. Thus, on the one hand were the two elderly Cooper brothers, who possessed a fleet of three blue buses kept in what appeared to be a lean-to, hard by their terraced home. Home was also the base of the major partner, a Mrs Bingley who dwelled in a farm-style property in Upton. The centre of operations was the kitchen of that building where orders were issued to the staff, and where conductors or one-man-drivers paid in their takings over the domestic table. Mrs Bingley was assisted by her middle-aged daughter, and so Personnel Departments and offices full of other staff members were conspicuous by their absence.

Basic operations were certainly the order of the day, and covered a route from Wakefield to Doncaster which followed the main road out of Wakefield to Nostell

When the PTE acquired the remainder of the Hanson business in 1974 it took over a fleet of 23 Ford coaches, this 1972 Plaxton-bodied example, seen above, BCX 425K, taking number 81 under its new ownership. A Plaxton Supreme II body was fitted to the Ford seen below. The former Hanson's operations traded as 'Metro Hanson' and in due course Leylands and Volvos began to replace the Fords.

In 1969 Hanson sold their bus operations to Huddersfield Corporation. Subsequently they also sold the remaining coaches. This former Hanson Plaxton Panorama coach is seen in the Metro Hanson livery after the operator passed to the PTE.

A United Services AEC Reliance single-decker is seen working the Wakefield to Doncaster stage service. This was a Bingley-owned vehicle.

Priory and then shot off to the right to travel via the villages of Fitzwilliam, Hooton Pagnell and Brodsworth. United operations can truthfully be described as utterly basic, and employed a very mixed fleet of 39 vehicles, the purchase price being £301,000 but the sale was not affected until 25th April 1977, once again after I had left the PTE. As the main Wakefield-Doncaster route seemed well supported the route should have been viable, but I quickly realised that country fares income would not support City operating costs. We will come to the result of that lesson in my thinking in due course.

Also to appear in 'MetroBus' livery after I left were examples from another of the West Yorkshire NBC fleets, namely that of the former Yorkshire Woollen company, which became incorporated as part of the 'West Riding Group', although retaining a separate 'Yorkshire' name on the vehicles. Seen above is a Leyland Leopard with Marshall 53-seat body, KHD 913K, which had been new in 1972, whilst below is yet another Leyland National, MHD 337L, new a year later. Both carry the WY/NBC-linked device.

# 5 – Goodbye Wakefield

**E**ven now, some 40 years since my time in Wakefield with the PTE, I find it difficult to put my feelings about the job and all attached thereto into words, but certainly by the spring of 1975 I was beginning to feel somewhat frustrated. I suppose it came home to me one day when, in my capacity as a Director, I called in at the Huddersfield base of Metro-Hanson to have a discussion with Gilbert Fox, the Manager, about the withdrawal of some more Ford based coaches and their replacement by more substantial Leylands or Volvos.

I found Gilbert in a very depressed state of mind, so I asked some questions to ascertain the cause of his misery. He then told me of the years that he had worked for the original Hanson owners and how, with or without its stage carriage services, the Company had always made a profit. But now, for the first time, with income roughly where he expected it to be but with greatly inflated costs, the unit was showing a loss and it seemed to him that there was nothing he could do about it. Consequently, had I any suggestions? I thought for a moment and then replied to the effect that sadly I had not. There was virtually nothing that I was able to do, and so my advice was 'Keep your head down, do what you have to do to the best of your ability so that you cannot be criticised on that score, and as you are not too far away from the opportunity, take retirement just as soon as is possible!'

I felt that I had not over-egged my position. Bit by bit, as the PTE organisation had grown, so had 'departmentalism' grown too, which was almost inevitable with a four directorate structure. As a result I had become a glorified Chief Engineer but the outside, and non-productive calls on my working time, were such that with perhaps one great exception most of my engineering input was provided over my desk once or at the most twice per week when Jim Pearson, the person designated with that very title, came into the office to share lunch with me and discuss how things stood. The exception came to be quite remarkable.

On Wednesday 25th September 1974 I rose early, called in at Wakefield and then took a train to London in order to spend two full days – actually I made it three –at the Earls Court Commercial Vehicle Show. It was approaching lunch time when I gained the venue, deciding to go first to the Leyland stand to see how our exhibit, Roe-bodied Atlantean number 6020, was looking, but my quick walk along one of the aisles nearly ended in a violent collision as none other than a Leyland Director and I met virtually head to head.

Apparently he too had only just arrived, so after an exchange of pleasantries he suggested that we went to the Company stand together, looked over the exhibits, and then went off to have lunch and a chat. Needless to say I was in full agreement, and so it came to pass. Number 6020 was immaculate in its show finish but what took my eye was a prototype 'quiet' Fleetline chassis fitted with the Leyland O.630 power unit. It occurred to me that introducing this sort of design into the city centre of, say, Leeds would be good publicity for the PTE (which was rather beginning to need some), but in any event it would give our engineers a chance to see what new maintenance problems might be encountered, working on the cautious assumption that, if it's new, it's problematical! One first question though was could we specify Gardner engines? The answer to this question was in the negative; the Gardner produced rather too many decibels.

It was agreed that on my return to the office I would send him an invitation to tender for, say, thirty; these to be additional to or a part of one of our existing Fleetline orders. I then departed to attend a meeting on the Volvo stand to look into the coach chassis order that was a long time coming. My letter was duly dispatched to the Leyland head office, only to receive an odd reply. There was no form of tender, but instead I was invited to a meeting with my contact at an early date to consider certain new developments, but these were not specified. It was all rather mysterious.

I duly made the trip into Lancashire and soon found myself seated in his office being plied with coffee, and then we got down to business. I was told that it had been decided that the Fleetline was to be phased out forthwith, and no further orders would be taken for the model. I should also note that the Atlantean was not going to have a long future either, when it too would pass into oblivion. Leyland was going to offer the integral Titan, which would be produced at the rate of 25 per week. Of these five would be erected at the Leeds works of CH Roe Ltd, the balance coming from the other and bigger group plant namely Park Royal Vehicles. This, of course, meant that the various independent coachbuilders would have nothing from the Leyland stable on which to base their wares.

I heard him out and then said 'This will cost you business' to receive the reply 'Where will you go?' I was, to say the least, somewhat miffed, pointing out that we had a considerable number of Fleetlines on order so why not stretch a point and let us have a few more when in any event no one that I knew had ever seen a Titan. But if a bribe was necessary, only I did not phrase it as bluntly as that, then I would recommend the PTE Board to take say five for trial purposes, and they could conveniently come from Crossgates. This argument made no impression however. There were to be no more Fleetlines period. So, being prey to dastardly thoughts, I politely refused the invitation to partake of another delicious Leyland lunch and headed back to Wakefield deep in thought.

By the time I had gained Metro House my thoughts were fairly clear. Of the double-deck chassis alternatives then available it was pretty clear to me that the Ailsa was not going to be the answer to the problem of filling the approaching gap. True, it worked, and the builders were picking up quite a few orders, but at the end of the day it had the configuration of the late and unlamented Guy Wulfrunian with its front-engined layout. True again that its engine was smaller, and so took up less space than did Guy's Gardner power unit, but would that smaller engine give as long a life as a Leyland O.680 or the Gardner 6LX? Then, one still had to accept a reduced platform layout, plus the noise generated as a result of the power unit's position. No the Ailsa was not the answer to an operator's prayer.

This left the Foden. But was Sandbach serious? Would the rather inelegant rear assembly and transmission design be somehow streamlined, as it were, and would considerable development work be put into improving its poor fuel consumption which could well have resulted from the engine to transmission

Two views of Leyland's Titan demonstrator working in Birmingham. The ugly rear end arrangement was to accommodate the cooling fan. The bus was largely designed to London's requirements and most of the type went to London Transport. Greater Manchester ordered 190, but in the end took only 15.

Volvo's offering was a forward engine model similar to the ill fated Guy Wulfrunian. Greater Manchester took one of the prototypes and christened it the Volvo B55-10, although it was to become better known as the Ailsa. This bus, with a Northern Counties body, was new in 1981 but was withdrawn as non-standard in 1989 and went to an operator in Fife. It was allocated to Wigan whilst with GMPTE and is pictured here in the town's bus station with the wires of the West Coast main railway line in the background.

characteristics. Well, as we have already noted, the Foden double-deck rear-engined chassis came and went in the twinkling of an eye, so it was just as well that no money was put on that horse. What was wanted was something brand new, but that incorporated some basic principles, so where did one start to achieve what then seemed to be impossible?

Once seated at my desk I wrote out a list of possible chassis builders who could have the capability of doing the necessary, studied the end result and drew a line round the word 'Dennis'. I next put in a call to Woodbridge Works, Guildford, asked for the name of the Managing Director and then requested that I might have speech with him. A gentleman came on the line to announce himself as John Smith and when I gave my name it was to be greeted with a definite chuckle. Mr Smith then apologised for the unusual start to the proceeding, declaring to my surprise that he had heard of me, and that in fact one of his Directors, a certain John Hood by name, who knew me from Halifax LoLine days, had become quite curious when he discovered who was calling. Mr Smith then went on to inquire how he could help me, when I made plain the basic reason behind my call.

His response was most surprising. It was remarkable that at this very time he had the other directors gathered in his office to discuss how a production gap in the works could be filled in view of the forthcoming completion of a

Government order for some quite complicated airport crash tenders. Now, buses as a replacement was, to say the least, intriguing. At this stage he would say neither yes nor no, but instead maybe, so should he come to Wakefield or would I like a trip to Guildford? I choose the latter alternative and so came to see a very different Woodbridge Works to the one that I had visited in LoLine days.

A goodly proportion of the premises were either closed or let out, whilst the extensive office premises that flanked the main railway line were also out of use. The offices consisted of partitioned rooms situated under the roof of what had been one of the workshops, and at first sight it was not very encouraging. Was this a concern that had any even remote chance of becoming a long-term bus builder, for remember reader that a PSV chassis in those days ought to be good for a 15 year life if it was built to a suitable standard. To buy them, and then to have to make withdrawals of vehicles with lots of life still in them because spares are not available as occurred with the Crossley marque when AEC turned the tap off, is expensive and is not going to do the reputation of the original purchaser much benefit if he remains in office at the time. I wondered. Still, the welcome was warm, and so we turned our attention to specification details. I wanted a Gardner engine, although at that time these were almost as rare as the proverbial hen's teeth, plus a front mounted radiator, substantial frames and transmission parts, and definitely no destructive trailing link coupling.

I also made it plain that the wheelbase, front and rear overhangs and the top contour of the frame should follow as closely as possible those present on a Fleetline chassis but this statement was then queried. My answer was to the effect that Dennis's reputation in the bus industry was non-existent and no self-respecting body builder was going to go to the expense of designing and then producing a new body design to fit onto a chassis that could be a flash in the pan. With the Northern Counties/Foden vehicle the situation was very different as the Wigan concern was funding much of the development but this was not likely to happen here.

Finally, I stressed that I would not wish to see any component – not even down to a nut, bolt and washer – sourced from a Leyland group factory which put paid to any thoughts of using the Self Change gearbox. Not that I had any such thoughts, of course, but my experience with the Volvo coach chassis had killed any such idea at birth. The net result was much more than I could have hoped for. Firstly, I would ask to meet with Mr Hugh Gardner, and see if an engine supply could be negotiable. This duly took place a little while later when Mr Gardner was most co-operative, our earlier spat seeming to have been forgotten. He viewed the Leyland policies with considerable concern, and did not wish to see a valuable slice of his business disappear overnight, so he promised there and then to start by making a 6LXB engine available to Guildford for installation and evaluation purposes if we reached the stage of actually putting a chassis together.

Secondly, John Hood of Dennis and I went on a continental excursion to try to see and test what alternative transmission might be possible. In Heidenhiem, Germany, the former home of General Rommel, we had drives with a bus fitted with the then quite new Voith D851 transmission unit, and were impressed by its performance and very much so by the inbuilt retarder that must surely have a beneficial effect on the life of the foundation brakes.

Thirdly, some mysterious characters began to visit sundry WYPTE depots where Fleetlines were based. They did not wear slouch hats and long black coats, but their identities were strangely never revealed. They questioned those in charge of engineering as to what views they had on the Fleetline, what were its good points and what its bad points were, and then all replies were carefully written down. When these preparations were completed pencils began to glide over paper and the Dennis design department came up with what I thought was an elegant solution to the rear transmission layout. There was, though, another step to take.

A redundant WYPTE Daimler CVG vehicle was dispatched to Woodbridge Works where out came the original engine and gearbox, and in went the new Gardner complete with Voith box. Then the resulting assembly was painted orange, when those who came to behold it were wont to call it either the 'Clockwork Orange' or the 'Denditch'. I will leave it to you, reader, to decide which was the most suitable. Orange or not, though, one thing was immediately very clear. The Gardner and the Voith might have been made for each other, their characteristics being so compatible. We were off!

The Clockwork Orange operating in South Yorkshire, running to Sheffield Lane Top and caught by Jeremy Green in this print which Paul Fox kindly supplied.

As work progressed to bring this new Dennis bus chassis into being, some talks were held with Executives of the Metro-Cammell-Weymann concern as Washwood Heath was naturally concerned about Leyland's future intentions, which soon became widely known. In the event, to the best of my knowledge and belief, no Dominator chassis (as the model was named) were ever bodied by MCW, the firm going on to recruit members of the former Daimler design staff and producing their own chassis and so marketing the well-known Metrobus.

Interestingly here Trevor Webster, the very gentleman with whom I had viewed the Leyland stand at Earls Court and who had told me in his Leyland office that there would be no more Fleetlines, came to leave Lancashire, joined the MCW team and so became closely involved with the design and marketing of the Metrobus.

Meanwhile, Dennis also needed someone to promote the sale of Guildford's new Dominator and so recruited Bob Crouch who had been the long-serving Daimler Bus Sales Manager and who had become virtually redundant with the ending of Daimler production at Coventry. He soon showed that he could sell them as well as he had sold Fleetlines in the good old days. Leyland's chickens were coming home to roost, and that regrettable decision was going to cost them business. If only Fleetline sales had continued until the Titan, and the subsequent independent Olympian chassis had proved themselves, history would almost certainly have been different – but then history is littered with 'ifs'.

Sadly too, no Dominator-based bus ever came to figure in the WYPTE fleet list as before the first example had taken the road I had left Wakefield for Leicester and my successor, having had his initial training with Leyland Motors, not unnaturally looked with more favour than I had done on the products of his old firm.

My departure was prompted by quite a number of reasons. As I said, I was in effect the fleet engineer with some added but perhaps nebulous responsibilities, which were not of sufficient magnitude to let me influence events. I was sure that a day of reckoning would arise in due course, and when it did those on the Board could well find themselves in difficult situations. Tom Lord and John Rostron could then jump ship and vanish into retirement, a luxury I did not possess. Not that I blame John Rostron in any way for the problems that were shaping up. John was by no means enamoured with life in the PTE and I well remember a conversation I had with him late one afternoon on the main street of Huddersfield when he revealed his frustration to me, and how he had just about had enough.

I came to the conclusion that job-satisfaction was worth a lot more than the apparent blessings of a high salary, so when the Leicester job vacancy appeared in the trade press I put in my application despite the fact that if I was successful I would be taking up a post with a lower salary. I must, however, add that so far as I was concerned, my relationship with our Director General was of an ongoing high order. We never had any cross words at any time during our time together, except in one rather perhaps unusual regard, and he had stood back and let me continue as a member of the Executive Committee of APPTO so that I would succeed as Vice Chairman for the year 1974/75 when by virtue of his seniority he could have claimed the seat, and no doubt the Vice Chairman's role, so now for the exception.

As I have said Monday was Board day, when the five Directors plus the Secretary and his deputy foregathered at around ten of the clock, facing a cup of coffee and those 30 or so items on the Board agenda. Discussion on various planes followed until about noon when the Chairman and Vice Chairman of the PTA appeared to have lunch with us, and chew over things of mutual interest, when drinks would be served (pink gins featuring prominently). Wine was also available to help wash down what was always a very acceptable meal produced in-house.

It was back, afterwards, to the Board table until four in the afternoon when Tom would exclaim "Frank the sun is over the yard arm". Our assistant Secretary, Frank Rowlands, would then go to the cabinet, take out a bottle of whisky, place it by our DG and add a tumbler, and a jug of water. Tom would pour out some firewater, add a modicum of $H_2O$ and I would sigh internally. We could then be in for a long session as Tom loved to relax, drink and pontificate before an audience when, as time wore on, his personality could undergo quite a change, not always for the better either.

And time did wear on as he would never rise from the table until substantial inroads had been made into the contents of the bottle. Initially, until I realised just what time all this could take, I stayed, and as I was more or less obliged to drink something, I made sure, and please don't laugh here, that a large bottle of Dandelion and Burdock was always available. I stood just a few of these evening encounters but then firmly resolved that 6.00 pm was my finishing time, when I would rise, bid the company goodnight, and leave the Board Room to the growls of disapproval from my Chief who would express the opinion that I really was an unsociable cove.

I cannot let the above remarks pass without due qualification though. Tom Lord was a remarkable man with a very acute brain when he chose to employ it, as is witnessed by his subsequent activities. After retirement he moved to a flat in St Annes-on-Sea and there began to take a series of Open University courses – ceasing to drink all the while – and it was there that I would go to see him as the opportunity arose. He first took a degree, and then obtained a Doctorate when, had it not been for his wife's illness which prevented him from completing the necessary formalities, which would have involved frequent trips to London, Thomas Lord would have become Thomas Lord, Barrister-at-Law, and it is in this capacity and for his overall friendship that I pay due tribute to his memory. Let us though return to 1975.

A former Halifax Albion Nimbus climbs the hill from Hazelhead Bridge on the Sheffield to Huddersfield road. The bridge in the background once carried the long abandoned Woodhead railway line, but is now a footpath.

I had the nasty feeling that our financial situation was not what it might be, and one gained the impression from time to time that relationships with the PTA were to say the least fragile. At one such gathering Tom was coming under pressure, being faced with a series of awkward questions, when I entered the discussion and relieved the situation something, for which Tom later thanked me. But here I confess these many years later that this was the only time in my long career that I deliberately gave my governing body an answer that was factually incorrect, and I vowed then and there that there would never be another such occasion. I gave more and more thought to the situation in which I found myself, and wondered for the future but I had no idea as to just how bad things were.

Eric Moorhouse, the Personnel Manager, some while later also became disillusioned with life at Wakefield, and applied for the post of General Secretary to the Employers side of the National Joint Industrial Council, or simply the Employers Federation, to which I have made reference earlier in this series. I was at the time Vice Chairman of that body and so along with our Treasurer, Royston Jenkins, the Transport Manager of Reading, was able, recognising Eric's sterling negotiating abilities, to offer him the post. He had kept a file of interesting papers which was passed to me after his death on 7th July 2008. In it was a copy of a report that appeared in the Guardian on 17th June 1982 that outlined the findings of some American Consultants who had been recruited by the PTA at a cost of £122,000 to assess the financial situation of the PTE. This revealed that in September 1980 the PTE was on the verge of bankruptcy, being just six weeks away from being unable to cover the wages bill.

The damming report seen in the national press confirming that all our fears had been justified.

# Transport executive could save millions, say consultants

By Michael Parkin

A report by American transport consultants has shown West Yorkshire County Council how it could improve its public transport to provide an annual saving of between £6 million and £9 million after five years, the leader of the council, Councillor John Gunnell, said yesterday.

He said the report, which cost £122,000, contained "devastating criticisms" of the performance of the county's passenger transport executive.

In September 1980 West Yorkshire's Passenger transport executive was on the point of bankruptcy, only six weeks away from being unable to pay its employees, he said.

The report, showed that West Yorkshire had the most expensive urban fares structure in Britain. In eight years there had been 11 fare increases, leading to a 39 per cent loss of bus passengers.

Of the three fare rises imposed when the Conservatives were in power in 1980, one of the consultants had said: "One rise might have had some merit, but taken as a whole, as a policy it has been disastrous."

The Labour majority, Mr Gunnell said, would not change fares before April 1983, at the earliest. That would mean extending the present fare freeze to at least two and a half years.

When new fares were brought in passengers would still be able to buy tickets in advance at the old rates. The new fares would not come into force until multi-journey ticket cancellers had been fitted to all buses, at a total cost of about £2 million.

The consultants would like to see advance bus tickets sales in shopping centres, at bus stations, and in the street from slot machines.

The report showed that the executive had no proper management information systems, had not developed policy options for councillors, and had no coherent capital plans.

Councillor Gunnell said he and his colleagues had to "dig and dig again" to get firm answers from the PTE on budgetary questions. It was not that management did not want to give firm answers, but that it could not.

Nor did the council receive necessary financial information from the National Bus Company. This year the county council was paying £14.12 million for the direct services of the NBC in West Yorkshire; last year it paid £7.7 million after receiving an original request for only £682,000.

For years the PTE had failed to get its auditors to investigate these payments.

In eight years there had been eleven fares increases leading to the highest urban fares in the country. The report went on to add that the PTE had no proper management information system, whilst the then Chairman of the PTA said that his Authority could not get any budgetary information from the PTE, and it was not because the Directors were refusing to give firm answers but they were simply incapable of so doing. There was also some doubt as to the true position regarding the claims being made by the NBC for services operated by its local companies on behalf of the PTA. In the year mentioned they totalled no less than £14,120,000 against the much lower £7,700,000 provided the previous year with the PTE having failed to have the books of the NBC concerns investigated by its auditors. It was all a very sobering story and thank goodness I was not then in a position of being held responsible in part as a Board Director for the ensuing mess. So who was? That is a question I cannot answer but by this time there had been some significant changes in top brass.

It became fairly obvious from day one that Tom was not exactly interested in the long term future of the PTE, and I wondered during my 18-month stay just how long it would be before he hung up his boots and retired. When that day came, and it could not be long away, John Rostron would never be interested in making application for the resulting vacancy, which would leave two other Directors plus this scribe who could well be. But there was no certainty that I would be the choice of the PTA to head the organisation nor would I wish to play second fiddle to either of my two colleagues. Then, if I was successful, would it be possible to make some significant reductions in expenditure without fermenting considerable industrial unrest? Would all the problems be worth the resulting additional salary? No it would not. So I decided to apply for the first suitable municipal General Manager's job that became available and keep my fingers crossed. If unsuccessful I would keep on looking.

In the event I did not have long to wait. Early in 1975 I went to a meeting in London to find myself sitting next to Leslie Smith, who was then the General Manager of Leicester City Transport, and he came to mention in conversation that he was intending to retire later in the year. The net result was that I began to look for a relevant vacancy notice, and in due course this appeared in the trade press, so I sent off for a set of the necessary forms and then submitted my application. Not very long thereafter I received a letter telling me that I had been selected for interview as one of a short list of candidates. But mark here the word interview; there were in fact to be a whole series of them.

They were to begin with a Sunday evening dinner party to be held at the Grand Hotel, where accommodation would be reserved for those candidates who needed to stay the night. The dinner would be hosted by senior members of the Council and would be followed on the Monday morning by a more formal session that would be held in the Town Hall. The interviews would be timed and so arranged that all six of those on the short list would find themselves together in a group just prior to lunch time when that initial six would be reduced to two. The survivors could then go and find themselves some lunch prior to returning to the Town Hall for interview number two – or was it three – when various senior members of the Policy and Resources, and Transport Committees would engage in what might be described as 'Municipal Filleting'. It was all quite a prospect so I cried off accepting the idea of staying overnight at the Grand and, declining the offer with thanks, booked in for the night at the Post House.

Consequently, on the afternoon of Sunday the 22nd June, I left my Halifax home to travel the hundred or so miles to Leicester, checked in at the Post House, and in the early evening caught a bus into the City centre and so found my way to the dinner venue that was very naturally to take place in a private room. There I met the other candidates, had a single drink (non alcoholic) and when invited took my place at the table noting as I did who was placed next to who.

I took it all very quietly, saying as little as possible, and not offering any opinions on anything which caused one senior member of the Transport Committee to ask me what did I think of the Metro Scania and Metropolitan vehicles that were then entering the Leicester fleet in some quantity. I replied that this was not the place to provide an answer to the question, but if he would be so kind as to repeat it in private interview the following morning, I would be more than ready to express my views in full on the matter.

Eventually the dinner came to an end and the company split up, I taking a bus back to the Post House and having a good night and not having to find myself in the company of competitors at the breakfast table. I see from my diary that I was not due to appear before what was then the full Transport Committee until later in the morning so I elected to have a few bus rides, selecting a vehicle going rather appropriately to Halifax Drive and being surprised at the shortness of the journey. I then spent some time watching the buses loading and departing from stops around the Clock Tower and Gallowtree Gate, realising as I did so that the number of passengers being carried was considerably more than would have been the case in the centre of Halifax at those times on a Monday morning. I then reported to the Town Hall in time for my pre-arranged session when the gentleman I was later to know as Councillor Kimberlin duly asked me to give my considered opinion on those newly purchased vehicles of joint Swedish and Birmingham parentage, but I will save my views for later in this story.

One of the Leicester Metro Scanias which was the subject of a question at the interview.

Eventually the morning reached its close; the Members went into a huddle to consider what they had seen and heard and came back with their decision. I and one other were to return at 2pm for further consideration, when in the meantime we might care to seek some refreshment. It was obviously going to be a long session, as it was, but I found it quite exhilarating, even though feeling that I was bound to be on the outside track as my competitor had previous experience in various capacities with LCT whilst I knew next to nothing about its operations or its current financial performance.

The two of us were later joined by a reporter from the local Leicester Mercury paper who seemed to be taking the suspense as to who would win far worse than we were. Time certainly did drag on, but in due course the Committee clerk emerged from the room where the interviews had taken place to ask me to step forward.

This meant all things being equal that the job would be mine, but a little bargaining was now called for as the Leicester salary was rather less than the one I was in receipt of at the PTE, and whilst I was quite ready to accept a pay cut for the privilege of being a General Manager once more, I obviously wanted any gap to be as little as possible. Fortunately, the Members expressed some sympathy with my situation, did their best for me, and also agreed that vintage buses that I had in my care at Halifax could be housed at Abbey Park Road on the same terms and conditions as was the case in Yorkshire.

As part of the package of concessions I secured when moving to Leicester, my new employers agreed that my fleet of vintage buses, which included this Leyland TD1 painted in Halifax livery, could be accommodated at Abbey Park Road.

A starting date was agreed as I was subject to three months notice, and so I left for home to tell my wife and family that we could soon be moving one hundred miles nearer to our Torbay holiday home. Also Leicester seemed to be a much more pleasant city than others I could mention that were also located in the Midlands. Being as it was in a somewhat isolated position and not in a conurbation there was little chance of Leicester City Transport being swept up into a PTE. I had had one such experience and did not want another.

I returned to Wakefield the following day to receive the congratulations of my fellow directors which I duly acknowledged, and thereafter continued to play my part in the management of the undertaking in general, and the engineering side in particular, where two major problems exercised my mind. The first was to improve the fuel consumption and operating ability of our new Metropolitan double-deckers, which was doubly important now, and the second was to try to reduce anticipated expenditure of the Bradford Interchange which was now in the process of construction. This latter task initially involved deleting the idea of having the enclosed passenger area heated under its floor, taking out the originally intended garage signalling system, and deciding that the aforementioned passenger access doors that were to have automatic operation so that they would open as a bus pulled into its loading position did not.

What none of the PTE staff knew at this time was that my reservations about putting a bus station on the roof of a garage were to become reality, thanks simply to the boots of the workers that had an adverse effect on the condition of the waterproof membrane that was to stop any possibility of moisture seeping through and so dripping into the garage below. This and several other problems became apparent after the complex had come into full use, but by then I was firmly ensconced in Leicester and so was not involved in endeavouring to put matters to rights.

Looking back it was all too complicated for what it had to do. I worked through my notice, attending during the annual municipal conference which was held at Bournemouth acting as Vice President and finally made a farewell tour of our works and garages on my last PTE day, namely 30th September, and it was little wonder that my successor to the PTE Directorship moved out as soon as was practically possible.

Before I left the PTE I was able to attend the annual conference of the Municipal Transport Association or the Association of Public Passenger Transport Operators, as it was then called, when I was elected Vice President. But I was never to attain the Presidency, as by the end of the year the Association was wound up, and its former role was largely taken over by a new organisation within the umbrella of the Association of District Councils. The Employers Federation continued to survive, however, and on learning of my move to Leicester the Chairman of that body made contact and told me that I would be made one of that body's principal officers so I found myself as Federation Treasurer, once more involved in such matters as national wage increase negotiations, or as a member of a visiting Emergency Committee set up to settle some local and contentious issue. It was not an honour that I had sought, nor was I actually overjoyed when later I was appointed Vice Chairman, but there was one great benefit here. We had need to appoint a new General Secretary and so Eric Moorhouse, who had also become very disgruntled by life in the West Yorkshire PTE as Personnel Manager, made an application for the position and was promptly appointed. Eric became a tower of strength and continued in office for the rest of the life of the Federation. He was certainly a very skilled negotiator, and so took much of the load off Chairman Councillor Norman Harris and myself.

I finally cleared as many outstanding matters as I could, received a clock as a parting gift from my director colleagues and a pair of binoculars from my immediate staff and spent my very last day on a tour of our various works and premises to say goodbye to my remote staff and so came to leave Wakefield behind together with my company Jaguar. It was just as well that I relinquished the car as my former director colleagues came to find that they had to pay some sizeable tax bills by way of benefit in kind.

All I had to do now was to move to Leicester, acquaint myself with the operation and practices of my new undertaking and find a suitable house in a location that did not involve an 18-mile each way commuting journey to and from a house that would satisfy the aspirations of 'her indoors'. Rather easier said than done perchance!

The parting of the ways. Tom Lord, the PTE's Director General and the author, sharing a final joke perhaps, but both knowing that the presentation clock on the desk was ticking for the PTE just as much as it would for Geoffrey in his future, for under the surface the financial foundations were certainly no laughing matter as we saw on page 79.

# 6 – Hello Leicester

On Wednesday 1st October 1975 I started up my car and drove the one hundred miles or so to Leicester, arriving at the Abbey Park Road office by around ten o'clock to find the Chairman and Vice Chairman waiting in what was to be my office, in order to welcome me to the undertaking. This was certainly a very nice gesture on their part. We had coffee together and chatted over the current state of affairs and after about an hour with me they left, leaving me to start the process of bedding in. My first task was to ask the Chief Officers to join me for more coffee and another chat. I had previously met my deputy, Peter Goodrich, but not Frank Lincoln the Chief Engineer, Maurice Simpson the Chief Accountant or the Traffic Superintendent Ron House and several other senior figures.

Once these formalities had been completed it was time to take a walk around the garage and to meet the supervisory staff there, during which time Frank Lincoln tentatively asked if it was my intention to change the vehicles' colour scheme? When I asked why, the answer was that in his experience to date every new General Manager that had come his way had started by introducing a new livery, but I had to say that I saw nothing wrong with the cream and maroon shades as currently exhibited. These were a Leslie Smith innovation and so as far as I was concerned let them stay. This seemed to relieve Frank and so we went on to review the bus fleet which at the time of my arrival consisted of:

71 Leyland PD3s with open rear platforms.
23 Leyland Atlanteans.
10 AEC Renowns with open rear platforms.
3 AEC Renowns with forward entrances.
28 Bristol RE single-deckers with two doors.
35 Metro Scania single-deckers with two doors.
63 Metropolitan double-deckers with two doors.
1 Ford luxury coach – a recent purchase.

At the time of my arrival a further batch of Metropolitan double-deckers was in the course of delivery, taking the fleet numbers 154 to 173 to give a total of 63.

All the Metro Scanias and the first eight Metropolitans numbered 266-273 were fitted with the Scania $CO_2$ power unit, but all the subsequent Metropolitans had the slightly larger and so more powerful $CO_6$ engine.

The range of buildings that I came to look over was certainly extensive, part of them backing onto the canal and the other part fronting Abbey Park Road. At the left hand end of the former stood the high-roofed later-built bus garage, at the far end of which lay the inspection pits and the fenced off area where tyres were stored and the tyre fitters had their base. This building also accommodated the washing machine, which gave a good wash but its design was such that washing was a slow process.

On the far right were the fuel pumps, with a runway that allowed vehicles to gain the old tramway bays, but these were not sufficient to house all the buses

When I arrived at Leicester in 1975 the oldest buses in the fleet were 71 Leyland Titan PD3s, all with rear entrance bodies. Number 65, a PD3A2 dating from 1966/7, is seen above working service 14 to New Parks. Below 1969 Leyland Atlantean 96 with ECW bodywork is pictured in Uppingham Road on service 17 heading for Braunstone. ECW vehicles had been available on the open market since 1966 following a simple yet clever share exchange between Leyland and the Transport Holding Company masterminded by Bristol area MP Tony Benn, responsible for Trade & Industry in the Labour Government and also representing his constituents, many of whom were workers in the Bristol based vehicle manufacturing company.

Two of the batch of three AEC Renowns with front entrance bodies stand inside Abbey Park Road depot above, while Bristol RE single-decker 133, – like the Atlantean opposite – had also been bodied by Eastern Coach Works of Lowestoft and new in 1969, is shown below working service 75 to Beaumont Leys. The flat windscreens allowed a wider front doorway to be fitted without compromising the seating capacity.

undercover, so at night 40 had to be parked in the yard ranked five across and eight deep. These bays reduced in length as one walked towards the City end of the premises, those at the far end housing the pool shop, for LCT did far more than simply maintain buses. Every item of wheeled transport owned by the City Council together with numerous items of mechanical plant was repaired in the pool shop and without doubt the most malodorous were the refuse collection vehicles that certainly had a hard life. There were no less than 508 items recorded on the maintenance register.

At this end of the yard was the quite new purpose-built testing station. At first the Government required cars over ten years old to be subject to an annual test, but by 1984 the time interval had been greatly reduced to three years. During my first full year in office 10,437 vehicles had been inspected on one or other of the two test lines the building contained, but in my last full year the number had increased to 18,475. By this time a second station had been equipped within one of the existing buildings. The first station also inspected all the taxis and hire cars licensed to ply in the City (latterly 450) and the regular staff employed in this work certainly knew all the tricks of the trade. There was also a lawn mower repair section dealing with Parks Department machinery (600 items initially), whilst also at the far city end in its own building was what I humorously came to call the plastics division. Here glass fibre items were produced and the chemicals used in the work carefully stored.

The large building that fronted Abbey Park Road and carried the sizeable Leicester City Transport lettering had been built to provide space for tramcar repairs and possible construction. Now it contained the fuel pump shop, the body shop and, of very recent introduction, a pair of fixed vehicle lifts. Access to these was gained through doors which had been cut in the outside yard facing walls, and here heavy repairs were undertaken. This left the paint shop which was sandwiched between the later bus garage and the original tram shed bays, and this was perhaps the least acceptable of the premises from a working point of view, but there was nothing wrong with the standard of finish coming out of the shop. There was also a stores building closely alongside.

All the various departments had a long-service highly skilled foreman, and other engineering staff members were Mr Williams, the Assistant Chief Engineer (a body maker by trade), the Assistant Engineer who dealt mainly with pool shop affairs, and the Technical Assistant. It seemed from that first quick inspection that engineering was in good shape generally, but I did have to listen to a few grumbles as was only to be expected. Finally, I should mention that in addition to maintaining the City Council's vehicles the pool shop also repaired another 265 owned by various outside agencies such as the County Council. This was all big business.

After digesting this news I was taken to the Rutland Street Operating Centre to meet the Chief Inspector and several members of his staff, and to see the impressive range of TV monitors that let their operator see what was going on throughout the whole of the City Centre, thanks to their pan and scan capabilities. I also noted how every vehicle was fitted with two way radio, and how the air was truly alive with messages. The staff obviously had no inhibitions when it

Leicester purchased both single and double deck versions of Metro-Cammell's joint venture with Scania. In the picture above Metro-Scania single-decker 224, the last of a batch of 15, is seen on service 73 to Mowmacre Hill.

The double-deck version, which shared the same lower deck frontal style and trim, and also the same lively acceleration and matching not inconsiderable thirst, was christened the Scania Metropolitan, 286 being pictured on the left.

The final version, the Metrobus, was less sophisticated and more reliable. The aluminium trim was dropped and large numbers of this bus were built, including Leicester 37 photographed on the left en route to New Parks on service 14.

came to using the equipment. Finally I was shown my dining room which, as one of my colleagues later said, allowed me, with my oak panelled office, to dwell in almost baronial splendour.

There was a lot to take in that first day, but the day did end on an interesting note. My secretary, Mrs Irene Cross, came in with such mail as required my signature, waited until I had done the necessary, picked it up, walked to the door, paused and said 'It has been a surprising day, it just feels as if you have been here for ages.' With that she blushed and apologized for speaking when she should not have done. I told her no apology was necessary as it was to me a sort of coming home, being a General Manager once more, and so I had just the same feeling. I decided, though, to start off very quietly with no sudden changes in procedure, but after only a very short time any equilibrium that I might have had was rudely interrupted.

The Council's Chief Executive, who was in effect the Town Clerk of old with a new title, asked me to see him when he presented me with a voluminous report on the future of the Transport Department, which had been produced by the Management Services organisation. This suggested wholesale changes. The General Manager and immediate staff should be moved to the intended new council offices at the New Walk Centre, the Chief Accountant and some of his team should be incorporated within the department of the City Treasurer, Management Services would come to play a bigger part in the affairs of Transport and, of course, there were various other proposals intended, too numerous to detail here.

I scanned through the pages and was shocked, saying if I had known of the existence of this document I would never have applied for the job, so in the circumstances I could not pass any judgment on its merits or otherwise, and needed at least six months experience as General Manager before I would be able to offer some soundly based opinions. Actually, he could have had one instantly, but that could have been very counterproductive. Our Chief Executive was a reasonable colleague and so agreed with my softly spoken contention, saying that the issue would not be pressed and it was not. The six months duly went by, and the Transport Department continued as of old as we went on without any wave-making incidents. No one raised the subject of that report until there came the blessed day, when, asked about it by a Member of the Council in Committee, one of the authors denied that any such document had ever been written!

One needs to have luck on one's side, but I suspect that here was an attempt to restrict the activities of my predecessor who was certainly a free spirit, and whose transport researches took him to such places as San Francisco and all the major European cities. I withdrew from membership of the International Transport Union (UITP) and so spent most of my time within these shores, but as you will see there came to be at least one very interesting exception.

To return though to 1975/76. Financial matters figured largely in my daily round and I had, of course, arrived in the middle of the financial year which was to end on 31st March 1976. At 31st March 1975 a trading surplus of £64,604 was recorded, to which could be added the profit from the excellent car testing station at Abbey Park Road and interest generated on existing funds. This resulted in a

When I arrived in Leicester the fleet contained only a small number of Leyland Atlanteans, 23 in total, and the final delivery of 10 in 1969 had been bodied by Park Royal with their distinctive sloping back upper front windows and frowning peak.

The body shop in Abbey Park Road works, with another of these Leyland Atlanteans receiving attention to its front dash panel, while a Metro Scania single-decker stands in the background.

figure of plus £80,170 but then the useful sum of £120,000 was transferred to the bus renewals fund, leaving a deficit of £39,830 to be funded from reserves.

By the 31st March 1976 the deficit had increased to £146,989. This was after £270,000 had been allocated to the bus renewals fund, £72,000 to the insurance fund as LCT carried its own insurance risks, and £28,809 to miscellaneous capital expenditure matters, so the position could have been a lot worse. There had been some quite substantial wage awards made by the national bodies during the year and to offset these fares increases had been introduced on 17th September 1975 and again on 1st February 1976. Various economies were also made, with Sunday mileage being reduced by 5.7% of that scheduled or 958 miles in total but conversely a new service to the intended large estate being built at Beaumont Leys was introduced on the 1st December 1975.

So we came to enter 1976/7, the staff level having fallen from 912 to 861, and I had fought another successful battle. The Council elections were looming and the ruling Labour group was concerned that it could well lose control of the Council when the results were declared. A meeting took place at Rutland Street with the Leader of the Council, the Chairman, the Vice Chairman, and certain other important members. The suggestion was then raised that money might be taken from the sizeable sum then figuring in the Bus Renewals fund to support the undertaking, when no unpopular fares increase would then be necessary. Rather rashly I argued that this bordered on the immoral.

We paid cash for new vehicles, thus avoiding heavy loan charges that in the end would come to bear on future passenger charges, and it did not matter to me what political party was advancing this sort of theft, I would and must be dead against it. My Chairman, who had heard this argument before, turned to the Leader and said "Well, I told you what his reaction would be." The leader, who was in fact a clergyman of the Church of England and a man whom I had come to like, pondered for a moment and then closed the meeting saying he would let me have an answer the following day. He was as good as his word and then said "Your Bus Renewals fund will stay untouched, there can be a fares increase, and if we lose the election you know who will be to blame!"

I don't know if I was or I was not, but lose the party did and with the new Conservative administration came a new mandate; 'That the affairs of the Transport Undertaking should be so ordered as to reduce to a minimum the possibility of a deficit arising which would have to be funded by the General Rate fund.' Interesting times ahead perchance!

The subject of new buses now came up and I decided to make some major specification changes. All our one-man vehicles had two doors and were fitted with Videmat machines, positioned hard by the front entrance. The idea was to reduce boarding times. A passenger could deposit his fare in the machine which printed out a ticket bearing a reproduction of the inserted coins. So far so good, but the driver on such occasions could not ask for the intended destination, and so did not know if the proper fare had been tendered or even if legal coinage had been inserted instead of a collection of miscellaneous washers. Collections of washers and foreign coins came to hand daily. Then, too, the passenger intent on defrauding the undertaking could leave by the centre exit doors and so escape driver scrutiny entirely. So scrap the Videmats, and buy bus bodies that had only a single front entrance.

Consequently, an order was placed for five more Metropolitans, with single doors, and what I hoped was an improved internal appearance, with moquette-covered lower saloon seats, and a level floor; all existing buses had a central gangway step. MCW here in my view rose to the occasion and these certainly were very well finished buses, which led me to write and congratulate the makers on the end result. At the end of the day though, like other Metropolitans, they came to suffer from excessive rear framing corrosion problems. These buses eventually came into service in November 1977 as fleet numbers 174-8, but with that order went another. I had not forgotten the association I had begun to foster with the principals of the Dennis concern and to further this, we had had the Clockwork Orange (or Denditch) running on extensive tests in Leicester. Now, after having seen the first completed rear-engined double-deck Dominator and tested it, a batch of nine were ordered.

Of these seven were to have East Lancashire single front-entrance bodies, again to an improved standard of interior finish, the first of the batch 233 to 239 being ceremoniously handed over to the undertaking and so entering service on 28th October 1977. They were fitted with body frames 'diverted' from an East Lancs order for fitting to Leyland Group chassis, Arthur Danson being incensed by Leyland's intention to axe Fleetline and Atlantean chassis. Fortunately, the General Manager of the undertaking involved never found out why his buses were mysteriously delayed. The other two vehicles, which became fleet numbers 231 and 232, struck an even newer note as they came to receive the first ever Marshall-built double-deck bodies, they too being similarly handed over on 1st October 1978.

The Dennis chassis price was £19,565, the East Lancs body £15,477 whilst the Marshall bodies cost £15,450 which was certainly competitive, but I was rather disappointed by the appearance of these buses which I felt had a rather old fashioned look that we could with more effort have improved. As was to be expected the 6.7mpg fuel consumption of the Gardner engine was an improvement on that of the Metropolitans at 5.5mpg, but the reasons were obvious. The Scania based vehicles had a transmission system that could be likened to that adopted by Leyland for its pre-war so called Gearless buses. One started off with the drive being taken through a torque converter until a suitable speed of about 19mph on the level was attained then top gear came in automatically. On the Leyland a lever had to be moved to make the selection manually by the driver.

The Voith transmission of the Dennis bus also incorporated a torque converter start, but now at a lower speed an intermediate gear ratio came in, cutting out the converter, which is never fuel-efficient. Then, when speed had been raised, top gear again cut in, giving direct drive as on the Metropolitan. The Voith, though, also incorporated an inbuilt retarder, so press the brake pedal and three stages of brake came in meaning the foundation brakes were not used until road speed was down to about eight miles per hour, which not only gave drivers a considerable feeling of confidence but also offered two extra benefits. Firstly, brake lining usage was greatly reduced and, secondly, the retarder was cooled by the engine

Number 233, the first of a long line of East Lancashire bodied Dennis Dominators, is handed over to the Lord Mayor of Leicester, Bert Baker by John Smith, Managing Director of Hestair Dennis, at a ceremony in Abbey Park Road depot in October 1977.

coolant so keeping the power unit nice and warm even if one was descending a lengthy gradient. This did a power of good for the heaters on a cold morning, and here we come to one of those amusing and quite unexpected transport events.

At the end of every Transport Committee meeting it was the practice for the Chairman to ask if any Member wished to put a question to the General Manager, when one never knew what to expect. On this occasion that question by the Chairman was duly put, and the gentleman who had been the Vice Chairman during my first days in office said that he wished to avail himself of the opportunity. He then said. "Mr Manager, I travel to and from work by bus every day, and this cold morning one of the Dennis buses turned up. It was so very warm, far different from the usual Leyland, so can you please do anything to bring the Leylands up to the same standard?" I replied that I could not, outlining the difference between the two models, and giving a brief description of the retarder that was incorporated in the Dennis design and how it had a beneficial effect on the heaters.

This response, though, did not satisfy my questioner, who asked, "Is there really nothing you can do?" "Well," I said "we could buy some more Dennis buses as we have sufficient funds available for the purpose." "How many could we buy?" asked Howard. So, not wanting to over egg the pudding, I suggested five. He instantly said "I so move." The Chairman, obviously bemused by this said, "Anyone second?" to receive an instantaneous "I do" from another member. "All those in favour?" said the Chairman "please show." All hands went up. "Anyone against?" came the next question. There were none. The Chairman then said "Well that's carried" and so it came to pass.

The next two Dominators carried Marshall bodies and were numbered 231 and 232. These were handed over at a ceremony a year later on 1st October 1978 and here Lord Mayor Albert Watson. receives the registration documents for the first-ever Marshall double-deckers. Chairman Terry Harris is on the right of the Lord Mayor with Chief Engineer Frank Lincoln to his right. Dennis Engineering Director Don Plumbley is on the front row in the light coloured suit. Bearded former Vice Chairman Howard Baker is to his right with Sales Director Bob Crouch between them.

Our wonderful, and at all times helpful, City Treasurer, who was sitting next to me, never said a word but after the meeting had ended he suggested that I had got away with administrative murder and he shuddered to think of the effect this minute could come to have on standing orders, but the only end result was the future appearance of that lucky batch of buses.

For vehicles based on a brand new design, we had few teething problems, but one we did have concerned those foundation brakes. Thanks to the retarder they suffered little lining wear, as I have said, but when a reline was necessary setting up the shoes inside the drums was very difficult. The braking assembly was of Girling manufacture and the supplier did not seem able to come up with a satisfactory solution, although once set up braking efficiency was not a cause for concern. Dennis came to appreciate the problem and only the early batches of Dominator came to suffer similarly, later vehicles being fitted with 'S' cams and an easy

Dominators in service. Whilst most of the Leicester Dominators were bodied by East Lancashire Coachbuilders of Blackburn, as shown by 190 above, one small batch were bodied by Marshalls of Cambridge with that company's distinctive bodywork as seen by number 228 below. Marshall double-deckers were rare, this being their first attempt at moving from their traditional single-deck market. They soon returned to that market.

adjustment facility. On the other hand Metropolitans ran off brake linings at quite a rate, doubtless in part due to their speed capabilities and driver enthusiasm.

In the event the financial year 1976/7 saw only four new vehicles taken into stock, these consisting of a like number of Leyland Leopard PSU3C/4R chassis carrying Willowbrook Spacecar 49-seat luxury coachwork, a purchase which I came to regret but they were my choice. As fleet numbers 12-15 they entered service on 26th November 1976. I had purchased bodies from Willowbrook in my Halifax days and had been very satisfied with the product, but the control of the Company had changed and so it was unusual to receive a visit from a member of the staff of that concern who suggested that all was not well within, and it could be to our advantage to ensure that we carried out frequent body inspections as construction proceeded, as we were able to do under the terms of the contract. We did just that, so the end result was acceptable, but I did come across a spot of obstruction. I went to Loughborough one day to find a Spacecar completed and ready for delivery so I suggested I might drive it home as Abbey Park Road was so close, but the answer was in the negative. No cleared cheque, no vehicle was the explanation. Eventually, after some argument, officialdom relented and I took the vehicle but only on the understanding that the cheque would be delivered by hand the following day, and cheques would be supplied each time we took another delivery. These vehicles cost £21,200 the chassis having five-speed gearboxes. A bus grant payment of £10,770 was duly received by the authority.

Delivery occurred in November 1976, but to return to Howard's question – when the orders in the pipeline had been completed there would still be 78 open-platform buses in use, together with three of the original Atlanteans which were reaching the end of their 15 year life span. By the end of the year the committee agreed by more conventional minutes to sanction the ordering of 16 more Dominator/East Lancs vehicles, and one with a Marshall body intended as a Commercial Show exhibit (but this was never built as Marshalls withdrew from the show) together with two more Leyland Leopards, only these were to be fitted with Plaxton bodies.

As was only to be expected in this era there were more wage awards, costing on estimate £169,000 in a full year, and these meant that fares had to be increased on the 13th February 1977, but it was possible to retain the 4p minimum adult charge. By this time another travel matter had received a good deal of attention. The Conservative administration decided that it could not continue to subsidise free travel for ladies over the age of 60 or men over the age of 65, there being some 31,867 passes issued at the time. A flat charge of 2p per trip (excluding the 4.30pm to 6.30pm evening peak period) was proposed and I was asked did I think it would make any substantial difference to our finances. My answer was in the negative.

The subject was duly debated at length in Council on the night of 25th November 1976, when the Labour opposition put forward all the arguments against such an imposition as one might expect. The ruling group did, of course, carry the day but after it was all over and I was leaving the Town Hall a very senior member of the Labour Party came up to me, put his arm over my shoulders, and said "I

Leyland Leopard 14, one of the four Willowbrook Spacecars, is pictured above working the North Park and Ride service. Although Dominators were now coming into service regularly, the bulk of Leicester's operation was still in the hands of the older Scania Metropolitans. Number 277, a 1974 model, is pictured below heading for New Parks.

do hope Geoffrey you did not think that we were trying to get at you. Frankly, if we had been in power we would have been doing just the same thing." It was a kindly act, and showed just how considerate the majority of the members of the council at this period really were.

Despite the foregoing, and a few arguments with Midland Red, we managed at the end of the year to put another £270,000 into the Bus Renewals fund, boosted by testing station revenue to £9,606, and carried forward a net operating surplus of £272,931 which more than met the administration's aspirations. But, before the year is left, let's look at the Scania-based vehicle problems that were detailed in my year end report for 1976/77.

Between the engine and the gearbox was a drive plate, intended to eliminate transmission vibrations. This was the size of a mini car clutch plate and possessed an inherent vice; it had some coil springs mounted peripherally and these broke all too often. The broken end could then act as a milling cutter and carve away the side of the aluminium cast gearbox; out then poured the working fluid and the net result was a very expensive repair. Drive plate life was never long.

The gearboxes themselves were not long lasting either. Life never exceeded 80,000 miles, with the result that during the year all 35 Metro Scania single-deckers had to receive updated boxes. With this change came the agreement that, in future, overhauls would be done in-house with the more problematical components being supplied at very advantageous prices. Several front axle beam forgings also had to be replaced.

The double-deck Metropolitans too had their fair share of troubles. High lubricating oil consumption had to be added to high fuel usage, and each of the 63 vehicles then in the fleet had to be given strengthened rear axle sub frames. At Scania's expense of course. The engines also had an internal problem that became manifest from time to time. They had 'wet' cylinder liners, and to prevent early corrosion a chemical pack was positioned within the cooling circuit that needed changing at the requisite intervals. This was not always totally effective, with the result that a pin hole would occur in the liner and so the affected cylinder had to be located and a liner change made, although the easy way out was to change all six just in case.

Now actually riding in these vehicles one thing that surprised me when I had been over all the bus routes was just how short in the main they were. One could almost stand on the flat roof of the office and see every terminal. The two longest were to Wigston Magna and South Wigston, which were worked jointly with Midland Red as the result of a tortuous agreement made some years earlier. However, on 4th October 1976 history was made when the number 30 service that had worked from the City Centre to Highway Road was projected from the latter terminal into Oadby. Introduced on an experimental basis and later made permanent, it represented the very first occasion when LCT vehicles had carried passengers beyond the limits of the City boundaries on an own-account basis.

Then on 21st March 1977 another service, number 76, was started to serve the ever-growing Beaumont Leys estate. Midland Red objected to this and put in an application of its own to do something similar, so recourse had to be made to the Traffic Court. Eventually, the Commissioners gave LCT a dispensation to go ahead, but it was quite some time before a satisfactory agreement could be reached. This converted that original out-and-back route into one of a circular nature, and meant that LCT had a very good chance of having most of the traffic that the area would generate when the estate was completed.

The next financial year, ending on the 31st March 1978, followed the pattern set by its predecessors. There were the inevitable wage awards, which, when combined, added no less than £343,000 in a full year to our operating cost, and so the equally inevitable request to raise fares were made to the Traffic Commissioners on 16th March 1978. However, as no date for a hearing was fixed prior to the end of the period, we went from the dates of the wage increase for platform staff in January and for craftsmen in February. They were facing an ongoing operating deficit of £25,000, arising in each four weekly periods, so for over a full year charges had remained static.

Only a few basic service changes were made in the year, these not being of sufficient importance to catalogue here. Intensive negotiations with the Midland Red management, which at times included County Council personnel, took place when I found the new manager of the Company, John Birks, easy to talk to. It could be said that due to having some common interests we actually became friends, which certainly helped to bring us to the point of reaching a number of agreements. LCT facilitated the moving of various Midland Red services from their remote terminal point at the Newarkes to St Margaret's Bus Station, nor did we object to the Company seeking to serve the Beaumont Leys periphery etc. In return, Midland Red's objections to our Beaumont Leys applications were withdrawn, and also the objections made to the LCT proposal to extend the 15 service from Coates Avenue to Tatlow Road, this facility coming into use on 10th October 1977.

I have already detailed the vehicles that were then on order, but with one acquisition not yet noted. This was the famous Denditch, registration number 9517 UA, which, with its work done, was purchased from the Dennis concern at a bargain price. Its engine and gearbox were removed to provide some very useful spare components and the rest of the vehicle was scrapped.

During its short operational life 9517 UA had carried a discrete advert reminding people of the Dennis concern's main activity.

My exploratory contacts with Dennis before I left West Yorkshire eventually resulted in the production of the Dennis Dominator and here the very first air-sprung Dominator chassis is seen before delivery to the body builder. It incorporates the later high driving position.

The combination of a Gardner engine and Voith gearbox, as I have said in the text, might have been made for each other.

There was though a concentration on improving the workshops and the equipment provided therein. No less than £43,363 was spent on the associated programmes, the major expense covering the provision of a large new tyre shop built up against an outside wall, and a suitable inspection pit. The old tyre section had been located to one side of the existing garage inspection pits. With the area now cleared further pits could be excavated, these having side or rear cut outs to make the maintenance of rear underfloor horizontal engines that much easier. Much improved lighting was installed and once these tasks had been completed it was possible to modernise the original pits. Our Chief Engineer was delighted by all this, and even more so when I agreed with him that we really did need a new washing machine that could give the buses a quick drive-through clean up immediately after refuelling had taken place. He was therefore told to go forth and liaise with his colleagues to see what sort of machines they used, and then having looked the field over, make a firm recommendation as to which one he would wish to see installed here. Frank Lincoln went off on safari and so found himself one day in a depot miles away where a new washing machine had been installed, and where the firm's sales manager, hearing that a possible sale might be achieved, had appeared with one of his minions to demonstrate to Frank just what this marvel could do. He and Frank were standing inside the machine when the Sales supremo instructed his assistant to operate a particular control, but the man pressed the wrong button. There was a 'swoosh' as the pumps started and the two persons waiting for the demonstration to take place certainly got one. They vanished in a cloud of spray, to emerge soaked to the skin. I cannot recall now if we actually purchased that type of machine, but Frank was certainly given a new suit by a very apologetic manufacturer and we certainly took delivery of an AVW Equipment Ltd machine. This was put into use in the May of 1979. I did rather naughtily suggest to our Chief Engineer that he might like to feature in an official switch on and wash ceremony, but I have to report that he expressed no enthusiasm to do so.

By the date that the machine came to wash its first bus we had passed the end of the year, recording a very satisfactory result. As usual, the testing station made a healthy profit of £33,567 our various monies brought in £26,634 by way of interest and after making another £330,000 contribution to the Bus Renewals fund, we ended up with a trading surplus of £184,206.

I must here, though, digress and turn to the office accommodation. The Abbey Park Road offices were built in the thirties, and the entrance from the main road was quite imposing. With its almost art nouveau doors, terrazzo flooring, chromium plated hand rails and sweeping staircase leading to the first floor, it certainly copied cinema designs of that era, and one only had to imagine the presence of a uniformed Commissionaire calling out, 'Seats in the circle, queue for the stalls', to complete the illusion. There had been such a person there located in earlier days but the post had been abolished for economy reasons during John Cooper's regime. The place had several faults, however, including that there was no reception area as such, so on more than one occasion strangers knocked on my door to ask the way to his or hers desired location.

There was an extensive basement that could be reached via the lift, but there was no downwards internal staircase. If one wished to gain the basement via one's two feet it was a case of going out of the back door, walking a few yards along the yard, and then using the steps to a door that led to the lower part of the building. According to Alec Barlow, the former General Manager of the St Helens undertaking but once an LCT junior, on the day of the official opening of the offices it poured with rain. The water ran off the yard and down the slope that ran around the building and down to basement level. There it built up until the basement was well and truly flooded, so to prevent a repetition firm measures had to be taken. The rooms on the other side were refurbished and then came to be occupied by the Chief Engineer and his staff. David Kent from Reading replaced Frank Lincoln when Frank retired on 30th September. Frank had completed 31 years of service, firstly as an Assistant Engineer and then Chief from 5th November 1959. He was the son of Harry 'Hellfire' Lincoln, who had held the post of General Manager to Wallasey Corporation Transport from 1923 to 1943.

The rooms on the first floor received double-glazing, suspended ceilings, and improved lighting. This floor came to house the staff of the Chief Accountant, Maurice Simpson, and so there was some internal rearrangement. The ground floor, to the left of the foyer as one entered, was occupied by the Deputy General Manager, the Traffic Superintendent with his associated staff, and the personnel of the Claims Department, so when all this work was completed the staff of each section was housed in the most convenient location possible.

To the right hand side of the foyer was my original office, and those of my secretary and the correspondence section. At the far end of the corridor was a meeting room and the men's toilets. However, these toilets could not be accessed from the main corridor; instead one had to pass through the meeting room, which could be truly very inconvenient. This situation was rectified quite easily and so meetings could then continue without unfortunate interruption. This room had been the place where the Members of the Transport Committee gathered before the usual monthly meeting, and there to be served with a pretty scrumptious cream tea. Once that had been consumed, they moved into the beautifully panelled Committee Room, and the Chairman took his place in the imposing arm chair located at the head of the table. These seemingly long-established customs ran for some six months into my period of office, and as you will understand reader, I was not unduly disappointed when the suggestion was made that the venue should be moved to the Town Hall pending completion of the New Walk Centre. All such Council gatherings would then be concentrated at that address on a permanent basis.

Once the initial move had been made, I moved into the former Committee room which was of considerable size. I then had half of the original table and my desk rejigged to meet the new situation. Now, in my new location, I could easily see what was going on in the yard, and also anything coming in or going out through the main Abbey Park Road gates. Thus, this was a very strategic location, but there was another less obvious benefit. It put some distance between my secretary and I, excellent though she certainly was. My original office had adjoined hers, the two being provided by an interconnecting door which in Leslie Smith's day was invariably left open, or so it was said. I had learned a lesson in the past, so I firmly told my senior assistants that I did not want my secretary to

Two vehicle types that had left the fleet by 1979 were the Leyland Atlantean and the AEC Renown. Atlantean 185 is pictured above on service 49 to Aylestone, while below Renown 36 is working service 65 to the General Hospital.

become regarded as my office door's guard dog. If they wanted to see me they did not ask her if the GM was in. They could either give me a call, or knock directly on my door, put their head around it, and say, "Can you spare me a moment GM?" If I was free I would wave them in, when unlike another place they would invariably be invited to take a seat. If I was busy I would reply by noting the request, and add that I would be in contact as soon as I could.

To return though to the end of the financial year. On 31st March 1978 the undertaking had a staff of 789 men and 60 women, an increase of 12 on the figure for the previous year. The bus fleet, including 4 Leyland PD3s awaiting disposal, was 237 vehicles strong, consisting of:

5 Bristol RESL short single-deckers
23 Bristol RELL longer single-deckers
35 Metro Scania single-deckers
68 Metropolitan double-deckers
69 Leyland PD3 open platform double-deckers
4 Willowbrook Spacecars
1 Ford Burlingham luxury coach
2 second-hand Leyland Plaxton dual-purpose coaches
3 Dennis Dominator double-deckers.

The balance of the order for nine of the latter was deliberately delayed as we wanted to have experience of the initial batch, just in case any possible modifications came to be required, but we had not at this early stage had to reline any of the brake assemblies and so had not come across the adjustment problem mentioned previously. On the whole it had been a good year but, of course, until the Traffic Commissioner held the desired fares increase inquiry, and agreed to our proposals, we were trading in that on-going deficit situation.

Fortunately, we received a letter to say the inquiry would be held in the Leicester Council Chamber in April when someone was, (to quote that famous Knotty Ash resident), decidedly 'discomnockerated'. It was usual for the Town Clerk's Department, to send an Assistant Solicitor along on such occasions to provide us with a watching brief. On this occasion though, they went one better, as his department had on its strength someone holding the status of Barrister-at-Law, that person obviously being fully acquainted with higher court procedure. Consequently, we had a meeting and I was asked to help draft out an opening statement. I said that was unnecessary, all that was needed was a simple statement namely, 'My name is…and I represent LCT, may I therefore call our principal witness?' Then do so and sit down. The Traffic Commissioner liked to move things on and never seemed over fond of long addresses. My advice though, was not taken, and the necessary statement was produced.

The proceedings opened and our Barrister stood up, to be quite ignored by the Chairman who looked at me and said "Good morning Mr Hilditch", to which I replied "Good morning Sir". "I take it", said the Commissioner, "that you are the principal witness in respect of the application?" I replied in the affirmative, to be asked to take the witness stand and then proceed to do my thing, a copy of what

I was intending to say having already been forwarded to his office. I suppose at this distance of time the whole affair took less than half an hour, when our proposals were accepted in full, and so the higher fares came to be charged from 30th April 1978. Our Barrister was later to comment on the lax way in which Traffic Court proceedings took place ; the first such hearing that he had attended against the much more rigid rules that were a Barrister's norm.

As usual, further wage awards could be expected to be granted at National level in the year ahead, but we were now in a period when the then Government was trying to curb inflation, and in so doing, restrict pay rises to a maximum of 5%. The resulting negotiations within the National Joint Industrial Council gave rise to some misunderstanding, with the result that a national strike was called. On Friday 30th March 1979 no LCT buses were to be seen in the City, an event that cost LCT some £20,000 by way of lost revenue and every member of the platform staff a day's pay.

Eventually agreement was reached, so, from 1st July 1978, office staff and inspectors received a 9.9% increase that was to cost £72,000 in a full year. This figure paled though before the £310,000 cost of the 6% on basic rates awarded to platform staff from 7th of January 1979. Then an award to craftsmen of 8% on basic rates became payable from the 4th February, which put another £80,000 per annum burden on our future finances. Fortunately, because there had been no fares increase for a year, traffic revenue had not suffered from a recession factor, the minimum charge remaining at 4p for an average distance ride of 0.62 miles. However, the charge for an average of 1.23 miles then jumped to 8p, which to my mind represented an undesirable increment, but as we wanted to keep the minimum 4p charge there did not seem to be any other alternative.

By 31st March 1978, the bus fleet had run some 5,993,500 miles and here one could make an interesting comparison as the fleet strength involved numbered 233 working vehicles with four Leyland PD3's awaiting disposal. By way of contrast, during my first year as General Manager of Halifax, the 168 or so buses in that fleet had run over 6,000,000 miles and encountered far worse operating conditions. Here lay the difference between almost 100% slow speed work in a flat City environment, as against some high speed rural and interurban travel over some very hilly routes.

Running all the then timetabled mileage began to pose some problems in this period as fuel supplies became very difficult, and there was an ongoing threat that we could be restricted to just 80% of our normal intake. At the same time – shades of 2011 – the cost per gallon (no litres then), steadily rose, so we had a leaking 5,000 gallon tank repaired, had it filled by virtue of 'the old pal's act', and kept our fingers crossed. Fortunately, these fears were not realised and so we were able to continue on the scheduled basis, but at times it was a close run thing. In actual fact very few service changes were made in the year but on 17th June another new route was opened, connecting the ever-growing Beaumont Leys area with the City Centre, travelling via Frog Island and Anstey Lane, the Midland Red concern making some associated changes on the same date.

The biggest upheaval was caused by the pedestrianisation of the Clock Tower area from Monday 3rd July when some stops and routings had to be changed.

The end result, though, was of benefit to LCT, as the scheme reduced the traffic congestion encountered there to zero. If, however, things were quiet in the traffic department, the same could not be said about engineering.

By the end of the financial year the two Marshall-bodied buses Numbers 231 and 232 had been delivered, but as that concern had been withdrawn from being represented at the Commercial Show, the chassis intended for the purpose was despatched to Blackburn, where East Lancs built a 17th body. All the attendant buses now came into stock together, with those outstanding from the initial order. To these were added two brand new Leyland Leopard/Plaxton dual-purpose 53-seat coaches, and these took the fleet numbers 7 and 8.

Despite the non-appearance of a Marshall-bodied bus at the show, LCT was still represented, with Dennis number 191 taking its place on the East Lancashire stand. By way of experiment, the body was given seats with moquette upholstery on the top deck as the standard leather or leather cloth material was very prone to vandalism. After six months in service it remained quite unmarked, so this material was specified for future orders.

We then did some Renewals Fund arithmetic and decided that we could afford a goodly number of new buses, so orders were placed in the year for the following to be delivered in 1979/80:

4 MCW Metrobuses with Gardner engines and Voith boxes, but we had to take two-door bodies
20 Dennis Dominator East Lancs double-deckers
2 more Leyland/Plaxton-bodied Leopards.

A wee while later another Dominator was ordered. To enable production to be as fast as possible, leaf spring suspension had been specified, and certainly the Dominators gave a good ride, but air suspension was obviously the thing of the future so Dennis went into a development huddle and produced such a chassis. Here was the reason for the additional purchase. With the arrival of these new buses, the number of open-platform buses still in stock shrank to 48, but in addition, the five short Bristols were withdrawn and sold to Blackburn Transport, whilst the totally non-standard Ford coach number 10 was also sold out of stock. Finally, reservations were made for the supply in 1980/81 of a further 15 Dennis East Lancashire double-deckers, and five more chassis of the same type that would receive Marshall bodies. There was also one other acquisition to be recorded. Metro Scania number 225 suffered extensive accident damage, and so was taken out of stock and to replace it came a similar bus, but with only a single passenger door and registered KHB 186L. This was obtained second-hand from the Merthyr Tydfil municipal undertaking in March. We then found number 225 was repairable so this went back into service after overhaul and became fleet number 10.

# 7 – Entente Krefeld

Nineteen seventy-eight was the year when I embarked on my continental travels. It was agreed that as a goodwill gesture we would present one of the traditional type of British bus, namely an open rear platform Leyland PD3, to Leicester's twin town Krefeld, in Germany. This had to be taken there, and because I had an outstanding invitation to make a visit, I decided to take it myself, recruiting my son Christopher, who was then the Rolling Stock Engineer with the Hyndburn undertaking known formerly as Accrington Transport, as my assistant driver.

The chosen vehicle, fleet number 85, was then overhauled and beautifully repainted in our cream and maroon livery, when departure was scheduled for around lunchtime on Friday 16th June. About an hour before this time it was stood in the yard, glistening in the sunshine, when in hurtled a taxi heading for the test station, as our vehicle inspector's for the station dealt with taxis, hire cars and various vehicles that came into the folds as previously mentioned. The taxi driver was going far too fast, skidded and crashed into number 85, damaging a side panel rather badly. The all-time rectification record then followed. The body and paint shop staffs rose to the challenge, the panel was taken off, a new one put on, and our infra red dryers turned up to full.

We left after a quick fish and chip lunch, about 30 minutes late. Then followed a smooth trip to Colchester, where we refuelled at the Transport Depot, and where Clive Sampson the General Manager presented us with some more fish and still more chips. We then set off for Harwich and the berth of 'Suffolk Ferry', a British Rail vessel that was booked to take us to Zeebrugge. We found that the customs man said he was having his tea, and so would not be subjecting us to inspection, so we inquired what next. The answer was to wait until a collection of railway tank wagons had been pushed onto the deck via the sloping ramp, and then our bus could follow, but now came a possible problem. The bus was too high to pass beneath the superstructure, so we had to park it about 2ft from the steel work and its back end was about the same distance from the square stern of the vessel. It was far too close to the sea for my liking but nothing else was possible. Once on board we were shown to our respective cabins and then led to the dining saloon, where, you've guessed it, we were served nothing less than fish and chips. The skipper, who was having his meal, was interested in what were we doing with the bus. We told him and he indicated that if we could drive a bus we could later try our hand at piloting the ship. "So come up on the bridge when you have had your supper".

Now the shortest route to Krefeld was via the Hook of Holland, but the Dutch authorities refused point blank to let a 14ft 6in high bus use their highways. The Belgians were more forthcoming, so we thought we might travel through that country, but on no circumstance were we to try to use a motorway. We were given a route map which on a casual inspection seemed to include every point of the compass, for the roads indicated on it could never be described as having the characteristics of a series of straight lines.

We sailed on time, in sunshine on a gorgeous evening with a very gentle breeze, and soon reached the open sea. I was then given the wheel and told to

The 'Suffolk Ferry' was a train ferry ordered by the London and North Eastern Railway but delivered to British Railways in 1948 for its Harwich to Zeebrugge route. Being too high to fit inside, number 85 was accommodated on the short open rear section, almost hanging over the stern. Despite a force 8 gale it survived the voyage intact.

proceed "in that direction" ie eastwards. Meanwhile, Christopher was having an erudite conversation with the first mate. He was then a keen member of the Paignton sailing club so was immersed in a discussion about ship design factors. The mate mentioned that with its flat bottom, 'Suffolk Ferry' was not a good sea boat. Also with the loaded railway tank cars now on board, it tended to roll over in anything like a sea, and then to speedily return to the vertical. At this point the Captain chimed in to say that she was built in 1948, the heaving and rolling was not doing the superstructure a lot of good, and he did not expect the boat to have a long life as a consequence. Not exactly news one wants to hear when heading for a cross channel voyage! He was right though, it didn't, and 'Suffolk Ferry' was scrapped in 1980. However, we sailed on, and then the skipper suggested that I looked at the wake which was similar to the lines on our route map weaving as it did from side to side.

The radio phone then squawked, the Captain had a brief conversation where he asked if I had understood what was said. I hadn't, so he told me that we would be encountering a force eight gale very shortly and so he had begun to worry about the security of the bus. In no time at all the sun vanished, we were in cloud, and the ship began to heave and roll. I stood it for about half an hour but then had to go to my cabin, lie on my bunk and watch my porthole curtains go from the vertical to the horizontal and then back to vertical again. Additionally, those fish and chip meals began to lie rather heavily. I felt ill, my condition being made worse by my thinking continually how I could go back to the Transport Committee and tell the members that I had lost a Leicester bus in the middle of the North Sea. Christopher was, however, of sterner stuff and so about 3.00am he was on deck with some of the crew trying to tie number 85 down. Fortunately, they were very successful, stopping the axles moving sideways. A substantial crash twixt boat and dockside finally marked our arrival at the Belgium port in broad daylight, and so the next stage of our journey could begin. Hurrah for terra firma!

Shortly after I returned to Leicester I wrote a full account of our travels, and this was later published in the Buses magazine. There is not the space to reproduce it in this volume, but some of the highlights just have to be detailed. On arrival at Zeebrugge we were met by a party of English-speaking members of the staff of Krefeld Verkehrs AG; we had a chat, they took our route map and then their car began to pilot us towards the German frontier. We began by heading towards Knocke sur le Mer, along a coastal road that was made up of large slabs of concrete laid on a very obviously soft foundation. The net result was that no one slab was in vertical alignment with its neighbours, and this had a very sad effect on the standard of ride. I was driving, and it was very obvious that the springs had suffered from the torment they had undergone during that rough sea crossing. Never before had I driven a double-decker that not only galloped but also possessed steeple chasing tendencies. It was a teeth shattering experience. Eventually, though, we reached Knocke and went on our way towards Ghent.

We duly reached the town to find it equipped with trams and tram wires, but fortunately our passage under the latter was not of long duration, and thanks to the measuring pole we had on board we were able to squeeze under the span wires. The next trauma was when our pilots must have missed a turn and we found ourselves running down a country lane which became ever narrower, until we entered a cul-de-sac that was formed by a pretty small farm yard. As we contemplated how best to turn the bus round in the space available, the farm house door opened and we were beset by a bevy of nubile farmer's daughters who were amazed by the appearance of this strange thing from another world. They were, though, very hospitable girls. We extracted ourselves from their company and farm, and made our way towards Brussels, a city that came to cause me a permanent loss of hair. There were tram wires in profusion, and all too often we were scraping the live wire. By now it was lunch time on the Saturday, and Brussels was very busy. Sadly, the tramway staff were not over-helpful when a British double-decker began to interrupt the smooth flow of the trams, but eventually we gained an elevated road, which was equipped with a whole series of overhead gantries. Number 85 went under these with almost no clearance, negotiating the quite lengthy structure, giving me some heart-stopping moments, but worse was to come. I can still picture the scene vividly after all these years.

There was a long straight road that with its cobbled surface, double line of tram tracks, and span wires resembled something out of Manchester in the 'thirties. The overhead line poles were planted about 12in from the kerb edge, and here the span wires were low. We could just pass under them, but only by keeping the right hand wheels on the kerb, and trusting that the lean of the vehicle would let us pass. I scraped past some of those poles with fractions to spare. At last, though, we escaped from Brussels and headed towards Louvain and Liege.

I had wanted to see the latter, having read about the way in which the surrounding forts had held up the 1914 German advance, until that army had brought up some monster siege guns to demolish them. Thanks to a series of

The Krefeld tram standing in the depot sidings after the naming ceremony.

low bridges etc, we had to by-pass both places following a whole series of very minor roads, all too often with very restrictive clearances.

Later in the day we ran into the village of Lockeren, which was a pity because the inhabitants were celebrating some form of festival, and the streets were festooned with lines of bunting. Now they may have had problems putting them up, but would have no trouble in taking them down. Number 85 did that very efficiently for them. At length we came to rest in the village square, where annoyance could well have become manifest, but instead out from what was obviously the best hotel poured a bride, a groom and a posse of wedding guests. In no time at all we were posing for photographs and taking the members of the party for demonstration rides around the village, when still more bunting suffered. Needless to say hospitality was dispensed, and so we came to leave the company in what I will describe as high spirits – and we needed them.

As it was becoming dusk we reached Eupen, and could see the German frontier only half a mile or so away, but, alas and alack, between us and it lay a very, very low railway bridge. We went into a huddle to decide what to do next, when a smart MG sports car pulled up alongside us and the driver asked in perfect English could he help. We explained the problem when he simply said "just follow me", and he set off down what can only be described as Salford-like ginnels, which must have been about 8ft wide, as too was number 85. A series of rather similar country lanes followed until we came to a bridge spanning a deep railway cutting, a bridge that looked to be decidedly suspect, as it was built of timber. Tired as I was, I climbed down the bank and tried to inspect the structure, but there was only one thing for it. The MG driver went ahead to prevent any other vehicle going onto the bridge as we were using it, whilst our German friends did the same rearwards; then with Christopher coming to walk beside the open cab door I engaged bottom gear and slowly, after taking a very deep breath, started to drive over it. There were, so Christopher said, various creaks and groans as we did so, (no, from the bridge, not your scribe). But we gained the other side, and from there it was an easy drive to a lorry park on the German side, where we left number 85 and settled down in the car for a speedy run to our Krefeld hotel. We looked forward to sleep in a bed that did not rise and fall every few seconds.

We went back for number 85 the following day, taking off for Krefeld in what was certainly a massed start of HGV's the second the frontier was opened. It was then a question of coping with their apparent 100mph speeds as we traversed the autobahn towards our final destination. There we handed number 85 over to Dr Brengan, the head of the undertaking, his colleagues and many members of the Transport Department's staff. We were then entertained to three very hospitable and enjoyable days, before we headed back to Leicester via the railways, and the Brussels to London Night Ferry sleeping car through service, where the channel actually caused us no disturbance whatsoever this time. There was though a sequence to all this.

Our Krefeld friends decided that they had to reciprocate, and so wanted to present us in turn with a Krefeld one-and-a-half deck three axle city bus. Arrangements were duly made, and so they left Krefeld in it on the late afternoon of Wednesday 15th November 1978, to travel via the Hook of Holland to Harwich. There we were to provide them with a coach, in which to reach Leicester, and someone to take charge of the Krefeld vehicle. On arrival in Leicester, the party was to be entertained to a Civic Lunch by the Lord Mayor and afterwards Dr Brengan would present the bus to the City's leading citizen. So far so good.

I awoke on the morning of the 16th very early; very, very early, and with a nasty feeling. So I rose, dressed, drove to the depot, and boarded the coach which duly left for Harwich. I watched the ferry dock but no German party appeared, so I began to look for them. I found a blockage in the customs hall that I entered to the consternation of the officials, so I had to explain why they, and the vehicle, had arrived in England. At last I gained their release, and they boarded the coach, but no way would Customs let the bus go too. I ended up in the office of the Senior Customs Official, and the argument began. He maintained that it had obviously been fully overhauled and so was worth a good deal of money. Consequently, it would need to be fully valued, a VAT charge raised, and when, and only when, it had been paid in full could the bus be released. I countered by asking what good it was except as a kind of museum piece. It could not be used on British bus routes as it was of left-hand-drive configuration and so had the passenger doors on the totally wrong side. I then went on to plead that it was a gift to the Leicester Transport Department and was due to be ceremoniously presented to our Lord Mayor at lunch time, so please could we move on. He was adamant we could not.

Number 85 is formally handed over to Doctor Brengan, head of Krefeld Verkehrs AG, after which everyone posed for further photos.

Doctor Brengen was intrigued to learn of the existence of a remaining Leicester tram, now preserved as a static exhibit at the Crich Tramway Museum.

Now early rising had sadly addled my thinking powers, but then the light dawned and fortunately I had referred in our conversation to LCT and not the City. "All right you win", I said, "so let's put the value at one million pounds". He responded by saying he wanted a VAT charge, but surely it was not worth so much. I said that £1,000,000 was a nice round figure, but it did not matter whatever it was, as transport undertakings did not pay VAT. He promptly turned to his reference books, consulted them, and then with a little bad grace indicated that I might as well be on my way with it. We shook hands, and then with a smile on his face, he wished me a speedy run to Leicester and that I reached the Town Hall with time to spare.

Well, driving a left hand drive bus on our roads, and especially through Cambridge with its all too many erratic cyclists, was yet another interesting experience, but in the end I reached the Town Hall with about thirty minutes to spare, and so all was well with the world. But now a second problem arose. We did not have a registration book for the vehicle and could not obtain one, as it did not fall within the necessary British regulations, so it could not be registered and then taxed. We did run it in the City from time to time on trade plates, but per chance this meant taking a risk.

One day, some little time after we had acquired the vehicle, I went to yet another London meeting which was chaired by the then Secretary of State, Mr William Rodgers MP. He had had some earlier conversations with me about agreements that might be reached within the National Joint Industrial Council, on which I sat as Vice Chairman of the Employers Federation. He wished to make certain that we did not offer any advance in wages etc, because that would breach the Government's requirements that I have previously mentioned. When the meeting ended he came across to me to ask how we were faring in our negotiations, saying he hoped we would not encounter too many problems. I said perhaps we would not, but I did have another.

He asked me what that was, so I told him about the Krefeld Mercedes and our licensing problem. He had with him a Senior Civil Servant, who then said, "You know what Mr Hilditch wants, Secretary of State?" I briefly pondered on a whole series of possible answers but his Chief asked what that was. His companion indicated that as SoS, he had the power to issue a personal dispensation, so Bill Rodgers, with a twinkle in his eye, said that here was the one thing he wanted to give me ever since he had taken office in the Department of Transport. We had a laugh and then the following day, as requested, I wrote him a formal request. I understand the vehicle still exists, and so I believe, there should be screwed inside the body work a framed certificate bearing his signature, saying that it can be licensed, taxed and run on British roads by virtue of his personal dispensation. As I have said before, it is surprising how often one needs a spot of luck.

Our luck was even better when we came to finalise the accounts as they came to stand on 31st March 1979. We spent £498,864 on those seventeen new buses, plus a further six double-deck bodies, eight double-deck chassis, and two Leyland/Plaxton dual-purpose vehicles, receiving £495,170 by way of a bus grant. A further £152,441 was spent on other items of capital expenditure. Operating expense at 91.9ppm, totalled £5,637,574. Revenue came out at

Krefeld's Mercedes one-and-a-half deck city bus which was presented to Leicester City Transport and caused problems for HM Customs and Excise.

The Author together with Chairman Terry Harris, Doctor Brengan, the High Bailiff and Lord Mayor, Councillor Albert Watson at the Krefeld bus handing over event.

95.8ppm, giving £5,878,202, when mileage run had risen to 6,133,879, with around 57 million passengers using the services. To these figures had to be added the 'goodies'.

The testing station produced a profit of £36,567, and another £26,081 represented interest paid on the Department's cash balances. I should explain here that there was an interesting agreement with the City Treasurer in existence during my time in office. If, for example, we could lend money on the market at 4%, it might be that the Treasurer needed to borrow some short term monies, but could well find himself paying say 8% on loans so raised. So he borrowed the department's coin and split the difference with us. He paid and we received 6%, a very fair arrangement that suited both parties. However, at the end of the day, after putting another £330,000 into the Bus Renewals fund, we ended up with a record surplus of £303,276. At my suggestion, when considering this situation, the Members of the Committee did not pass any resolution as to how the monies realised might be formally appropriated. So they were in effect left on hold against a possible and very unusual future event, but what this turned out to be will be revealed shortly.

There had been an earlier visit by a Leicester bus to the continent; to Strasbourg by PD3 164, painted and fully lined out in tramcar livery for the Golden Jubilee of Leicester's trams. But this one came back.

# 8 – More Leicester

**W**henever one moves to a new area you automatically come to meet people you have never met before, and this certainly happened to me during my stay in Leicester. One person that I met quite early on was a certain Mr Mills, which was not surprising as he had his office in the former National Telephone Company's exchange building (only that company was taken over way back in 1912 by the GPO), the building being almost opposite our Rutland Street operating base.

Mr Mills was elderly, an habitual snuff taker, and acted as a freelance transport consultant to some of the small bus or coach operators that existed in 1975 in-and-around Leicester. At this time, though, his client base had certainly shrunk since the end of the 1939-1945 war, thanks to various firms either selling up or going out of business. He took me with him, so I could be introduced to some of his clients, and one such visitation found me in Barlestone so that I could meet those running the Comfort Buses business, and also look it over. This had been started by the two Gibson Brothers, in the 'twenties, but neither by this time were still in the land of the living. The concern was being run by Reg Gibson, the son of one brother, and Graham Storer the son-in-law of the other. It could not be said that the offices and workshops were of an extensive nature, but it was a neat and tidy operation with a commendably smart fleet.

Mr Mills and I began to have something of a rapport, and so he discovered that I had a holiday home in Torbay, when he confessed to also having a rather secretive seaside pad that was within two miles of mine. Quite some time later we met up at his place, some off-the-record talks ensued, and when it was obvious that we were on the same wavelength more formal conversations began within official Leicester City Council circles. The net result was that on 23rd August 1980 at a meeting in Rutland Street, LCT acquired the whole of the Gibson company share capital for a payment of £231,000, this giving a value of £11 per share. For this outlay LCT came into possession of a large piece of land in Barlestone, the office and workshop situated thereon, all the stores and equipment, the balances contained in the concern's bank accounts, and the fleet of ten buses which were wholly owned (Numbers 81-90).

The existing Directors resigned and a new board was set up which had on it the Leader of the Council, the Chairman and Vice Chair of the Transport Committee plus two others, and I was appointed General Manager, being given a small but separate annual salary from that paid by LCT. I had, though, learned a lesson in my PTE days that you cannot run a rural bus service successfully on country loadings if you have to cover city-style expenses, so Messrs Gibson and Storer were recruited to continue to run the company as salaried officials, and were told that there was to be no interference from Abbey Park Road but rather do your own thing and retain profitability. It was profitable too. The main route ran from Market Bosworth to Leicester via Barlestone, Newbold Verdon, Desford, and Leicester Forest East on an hourly frequency to that rather remote City terminal at the Newarkes. A second less frequent service connected the same two terminals, but running via Peckleton. There were also some works,

Gibson Brothers (Comfort Coaches) of Barlestone was purchased by Leicester City Transport in 1980. Although only a small operator it had always bought new buses. Fleet number 29 was one of a pair of Crossley DD42/7s with rare Strachan bodies purchased in 1949. Both were withdrawn in 1962, long before the author came to Leicester, but this photograph is included here as it shows a view of the Gibson yard which was essentially still the same in 1980.

schools and market day operations plus a small amount of private-hire work, all the vehicles being built to the dual-purpose standard. It was a tidy operation, as I saw on that first visit, with all the vehicles being based on the then popular Bedford YMT or YRT chassis.

Shortly after the takeover on 5th and 6th January 1981, improvements occurred by giving later departures from Leicester on Saturday and Sunday nights, and also instituted a development that came to surprise me. The Bedfords were lightweight vehicles and were fitted with clutches and conventional gearboxes, but then two Leyland Leopards with Plaxton bodies that had been ordered by LCT were transferred to Gibson's and put into service as fleet numbers 5 and 6. They had, of course, semi-automatic transmission and large engines, being solidly constructed, but – surprise, surprise – they returned a better fuel consumption than the Bedfords. Gibsons' red and cream livery was retained.

There was also a surprising amount of village-to-village traffic, and to promote this we ensured that more bus stop signs and more timetable cases were installed along the line of route. Market Bosworth was now one terminal that I could not see from the office roof. We also sought to move the City terminal at the Newarkes to Bowling Green Street, but progress was halted when County Travel registered an objection although they had no grounds for doing so, so no improvement could be made until sanction became effective from 23rd February 1981. But another innovation was to come out of the ensuing impasse. As usual, LCT suffered during the year from increases in the cost of operation, and new vehicles plus virtually everything else, whilst recession had an adverse effect on passenger loadings.

In July and January, rises, firstly to the office staff and to the inspectors, added £66,000 and £102,500 to the annual wages bill and a 28.28 % increase for craftsmen on the basic rate (with a bonus abatement) dated from 30th December cost another £226,000 but this was dwarfed by the £625,000 cost of a 13% rise in basic rates for platform staff introduced from the same December date. As for fuel, which was free from tax, a gallon that had cost 30p at the start of the year was up to 55p by the end, and we also had to respond to a government edict that we could only receive 95% of the previous year's intake. Put both together and we had to say goodbye to another £150,000.

As for vehicles, a Dominator chassis rose to £21,082 and then to £22,264, and the East Lancs bodies rose from £22,242, to £24,898, all purchases being just to the standard specification. By the following year, when Dominators with air-suspension and the high driving position were coming into stock, a chassis was up to £33,654 and a body cost £27,548, and when one added £1,000 for the radio etc the final price per bus ran out at £62,202 so the amount that had to be appropriated to the bus renewals fund just had to rise year on year. It would have been bad enough if the number of passengers carried had remained static, but it had not.

There was an adverse financial outgoing of some £850,000 on the previous year, so to balance the books two fares increases had to be introduced on 24th June 1979 as mentioned, and again on 24th February 1980 after the Traffic Commissioner, fully understanding the situation, agreed to the last rise without holding the usual public enquiry. The cost of operation was now up to 113 pence per mile, but we had made some economies. There was some staff saving, and from 9th September evening and weekend frequencies were reduced by 8%. Life was getting ever-more difficult, but we were not the only ones to suffer in these ways and from July 1980 Midland Red began to cut back its operations on the Thurnby Lodge and New Parks services.

The net result was that at 31st March 1980 there was a £298,193 operating loss after £380,000 had been put aside to fund new bus purchases; this loss reduced to £200,154 after test station profit (£51,863), interest on balances, and profit on agency work had been added in. Compare that to the 1978/79 surplus of £303,276. We entered the financial year 1980/1 with the hope that we would experience better times, and I suppose that to some extent we did, promoting some new innovations. As previously mentioned, the high and ever-increasing cost of fuel oil was worrying and I wondered what could be done to affect some economies, thoughts that were sharpened when I received a visit from an old friend.

I had first met Peter Windsor Smith in my short stay at Daimler, when he was working there as the diesel engine development technician. He left the company to take up an appointment with Coventry Climax sometime later, but in due course returned to Daimler to become that concern's Chief Engineer. Peter had some very bright ideas, but by the time I had been in Leicester for some years he had left Radford, after Daimler became totally enmeshed in the British Leyland empire, and with a colleague, Ray Tailby, was running a small engineering business in Loughborough under the name of Maxwell Engineering Ltd. On

NOT TO BE PUBLISHED BEFORE 3rd JUNE 1981
_____

MAXWELL TRANSMISSION
fitted to
GARDNER 6LXB DIESEL ENGINE

Following the approach from Maxwell engineering, through the offices of the Department of Transport, as explained in the text, a Gardner 6LXB was linked with their new gearbox, as seen above. In the lower view a fitter shows the simple nature of changing clutch plates having merely disconnected the relevant airline and removed the cover plate. There was no need for extensive dismantling as the demonstration showed. Failure to develop the very simple Maxwell design is in the author's opinion one of the tragedies of British bus engineering.

this day he brought with him a drawing which he opened out on my desk and asked if I could find anything wrong with it. It illustrated a design for a totally new form of gearbox, intended to be fitted to rear-engine buses. It was simple, the gears were substantial as were the associated shafts, and it could be driven through a fluid flywheel so no inefficient torque converter here. The unique part was the way in which the gear ratios would be engaged via the medium of small air-operated clutches which were accessible through covers bolted to the outer face of the box, and so semi-automatic operation was easy to provide, whilst replacing a clutch plate was achievable without recourse to any substantial dismantling. The clutches also provided a retarder facility.

We wondered if it could be put into production, but that would take a deal of money and Maxwell Engineering was not a wealthy concern. Then I had an idea, went over the drawing with him again and asked if I might retain it for a few days, to which request he agreed. A day or two later saw me at the Department of Transport's Marsham Street London headquarters, sitting in a meeting taking place in those offices, and when it was over I asked the Chairman, Permanent Secretary Sir Peter Baldwin, if he could spare me some time in private. He could and did. I went over Peter's drawing with him, and told him of certain financial problems. Sir Peter was interested and in no time at all had promised to provide sufficient funds to allow six experimental boxes to be produced, and asked that Peter be in touch with him forthwith. The wheels turned and on Friday 22nd January 1981 Dominator 250 was returned to traffic after being fitted with box number one. Thanks to Sir Peter, the box was supplied free of charge, Dennis engineered the installation and testing began. As you will appreciate, our passengers were never likely to become aware of Maxwell innovation number one, buried as the gearbox was within a vehicle's chassis, but they could hardly ever fail to know about innovation number two.

I had been invited to a conference to consider the transport needs of disabled persons, and this came to be held in Kensington Town Hall on the 12th March 1981. The then Secretary of State had been scheduled to chair the proceedings, but in the event the Prime Minister required his presence at Number 10, so Sir Peter Baldwin stood in for him. There was the usual amount of chat, which finally came to an end in the late afternoon when we delegates were transported by bus to Westminster Hall where the Department of Transport hosted a reception. I was resting against a pillar, drinking a glass of Government sherry, when Sir Peter, seeing me, came across shook hands and asked how I had enjoyed the conference. I made some reply or other when he said that it was always the same, people were full of good intentions on the day and the air was always full of talk, but in the end nothing ever happened and it would be just the same after today. Perhaps, though, somebody would have a bright idea but goodness only knew when. I said I already had one, and at his request began to spell out the details, those being as follows.

Leicester is a compact city, set almost in the middle of nowhere, not being part of a large conurbation, so imagine a bus with a wheelchair lift and a rather specialist crew, driver and conductor having had the necessary training and first aid certificates etc. They start their day around 8.30 am and by 9 o'clock they are at an outer terminal point. They follow a precise route into the City Centre picking up disabled passengers as they do so. Then they run out to a second area and repeat the operation, covering different roads. On arrival at the Centre they have a break, and then take their initial passengers back home to return for the second group. Lunch break follows and two more similar runs are covered in the afternoon. On this basis we can do 20 workings over a five-day week, but it is never going to be a lucrative commercial enterprise. Special vehicles would be required and these would have to have access to a wheelchair lift by a nearside central door. One could not safely load or unload via the rear onto the carriageway, even if it was possible which, as things were at the date of the meeting, they were not.

Sir Peter, who was becoming ever-more interested, asked why not and was surprised when I explained the fault lay at the feet of his department for, as I understood the position, the Construction and Use regulations did not allow wheelchair lifts to be fitted to a bus. His reaction was instantaneous. "Could you start the ball rolling and I will ensure that we will issue a code of practice quickly which will eliminate that lift problem?" We talked some more and the die was cast.

The members of the Transport Committee enthusiastically endorsed the suggestions I put to them on the night of 14th April 1981, and so we embarked on the design of the requisite vehicles. Dennis had begun to market a new and lighter type of bus chassis known as the Lance, and this could form the base of the intended accessible vehicle.

Now I have yet to mention how bus number 90 came into existence, but I will shortly. Thanks to its inception we had begun an association with coachbuilders Duple (once Burlinghams) of Blackpool, and so an order for three was issued, but here arose yet another problem as the Government was putting limits on Local Authority expenditure and our capital spending allowance would only let us pay for the equivalent of one bus and a half. What can you do with half a bus?

Here again Sir Peter, when advised of the difficulty, waded in with his influence in Government circles and before long the order for three could be confirmed. The chassis were priced at £16,299 each, the bodies £19,970. With longer frames than standard, the complete cost when fully fitted out came to £37,233. Seating for 34 was to be provided, or 31 if three wheelchairs were carried. Eight standees were also permitted. Further mention will be made as to how they came into service so let us now cover the arrival of bus number 90.

I returned home on 5th February 1980 after what had been a long day, and told my wife that I was going to bed earlier than usual. I did so taking with me a book that she had bought for me that very day. I read about five pages when I heard the phone ring and then a call from Muriel to say I was wanted urgently. I galloped downstairs to be told that part of the depot was on fire. It was too! The steam cleaning bay was wrecked, and a Bristol single-decker parked on the lift to provide an early start the next morning was totally destroyed. The blaze was extinguished thanks to the efforts of the fire brigade, and I finally heaved myself into bed again quite some time after the break of dawn.

Late in the morning a Brigade Officer arrived to issue a certificate for the insurance purposes, saying as he did so that there had been an electrical fault. I disagreed. The bus had been in the depot all day, it was bone dry, and the employee who had put it on the lift assured me that he had turned off the frame-mounted master switch, and knowing his reliability I believed him. I would ask our Chief Engineer to see if he could find any possible cause after trawling through the sad remains, but thanks for the certificate and we will proceed to make a claim.

Our policy covered full gross cost of replacement; it did not subtract any monies payable to us by virtue of the bus grant, so now we could order a new vehicle. Dennis had now designed a new single-deck chassis with a rear horizontal Gardner engine, a Voith gearbox, and a dropped-centre rear axle. To help distribute the weight, the drive from the engine passed over the axle to the inside wheelbase frame-mounted gearbox, and then by suitable gearing back to the differential's companion flange. It was called the Falcon, and as so many parts were standard to the Dominator we ordered the first to be built.

What, though, about a body? East Lancs would build one for us, but a quick delivery could not be promised as a new frame design would need to be drawn up. Dennis, needless to say, were anxious to publicise their new model, and so included it on the Dennis stand at the 1981 Commercial Show, and there it was seen by Alex Gibbins and John Ruddy, Service and Engineering Directors respectively of Blackpool-based Duple Motor Bodies. John in particular said he would like to have the chance to provide the bodywork and went on to promise that if favoured with the order would ensure it was delivered in time to secure a 40% bus grant.

From 13th March 1981 bus grant would drop to 30%. Here he had another incentive to press on with construction as the Municipal Managers were to hold their annual meeting in Blackpool from 16th March, and so bus number 90 was duly displayed to the assembly, and received much favourable comment. With 51 seats and adequate standing room, the chassis was priced at £26,623 with a rise and fall clause, and the Duple body £20,055, so we were making a goodly profit on the deal. It actually went into service in Leicester on the 8th April 1981, just outside the year whose events are being described in this part of the narrative.

And then there was another event. You will appreciate that the depot fire had rather interrupted my normal sleep pattern, so by nine o'clock the following night I could hardly keep awake. I went off to bed, taking my book with me and began to read. I reached precisely the same line as I had previously when another phone call came, to hear my wife calling up the stairs "Phone call for you Geoffrey." I hastened to answer it, to be told that we had yet another fire. Well not quite! I have mentioned how 40 buses were parked each night in the yard, five across by eight deep. Now my attention was drawn to a vehicle right in the centre. Beneath a seat was a burned-out pile of ash where there had been placed certain inflammable materials, but the person responsible did not know that from my first Leicester body specification all seat cushions had to be fitted using fire resistant fillings. As a result, this fire had died because there was nothing that it could feed on. The police were called, looked the evidence over, and departed without saying much, until the next afternoon that was.

At around 3.00 pm I received a visit from a senior police officer who was accompanied by about seven CID men. The Chief told me that arson was regarded as a serious matter, and they would not be leaving until they had discovered who was responsible. I left them with the use of my office, and it's direct outside phone line, to attend a Town Hall meeting. I returned about 6.30 pm to find most of the officers eating LCT sandwiches, and saying they were miles better than those on offer at the nick. I asked how the inquiry was progressing to be told they were expecting a call from the Chief very shortly, and perhaps ten minutes later the call came. The culprit was now under arrest. A prison sentence duly followed but now came an intriguing fact. On every job application form were the questions 'When did you leave your last situation, and also the previous one and why?' In this case, if I remember the words correctly, were written 'Fire at garage and firm closed down after a fire'. Moral – employers, read application forms with care and wonder.

In addition to the new Falcon we had two more buses on display at the show. Namely East Lancs-bodied Dominator 251 and a prototype Scania double-decker that was delivered to Gibsons, displaying appropriate legal lettering. It ran from Barlestone for some weeks but in the end, to the disappointment of the producers, it was not purchased and then taken into our stock. Gibson services were further improved during the year. From Saturday 7th May 1980 a half hourly Saturdays-only frequency was introduced with one bus every 60 minutes going to Market Bosworth as of old, the other into new territory to serve Ibstock. Then the Sunday frequency was lifted to a bus every hour instead of two hourly with the additional service being extended from the original outer terminus to Market Bosworth station to connect with the steam railway. The extension started on 8th June, these improvements being intended to run during the summer months. Finally, on 28th March 1981 Gibson's Leicester terminal at the Newarkes was closed, all services being extended to Bowling Green Street in the City Centre.

Now I have mentioned that Midland Red had reduced their services to the Thurnby Lodge area and this was causing the local residents to make their feelings very plain. Several public meetings were held, when certain LCT representatives were present but refrained from taking any part in the proceedings. The situation was debated within the Transport Committee on the night of 10th June when it was decided to formally ask the National Bus Company if it would be prepared to sell the affected routes to LCT. Further to this, on 1st October 1980, the County Council approved a notice of motion requesting LCT to look into the possibility of extending its bus operations into other parts of the County.

As this came after the aforementioned Committee decision, no opinion was passed on the request. Meanwhile, several service changes had been introduced with buses to Stoneygate being converted to one-person-operation on 5th October 1980, and linked to the New Parks number 14 workings to provide a new through link which connected the Railway Station, the City Centre and St Margarets Bus Station. But economies had to be made, so from 5th October various peak hour frequencies were cut to reduce the number of buses needed to fulfil our requirements by 14 vehicles. As a result, by the 31st March 1981 staff numbers had fallen from 831 to 788, and the bus fleet had reduced from 235 to 229, but of the latter figure on the day the books were closed three Bristol single-deckers were out on hire to South Yorkshire Transport, as were seven of the once twenty-strong batch of later Atlanteans.

Fleet number 3, a Gibson Plaxton-bodied Leopard, is seen above on the Loughborough service run jointly with County Travel. Gibson's two former owners, Reg Gibson and Graham Storer, stand in front of the vehicle. Below, in pristine condition, new Dennis Dominator 248 works the former Gibson service to Ibstock.  And who, you may ask, is that man with the camera?

The financial year 1980/81 saw substantial changes in the composition of the two bus fleets, Gibsons and LCT. Two more Leyland Leopard/Plaxton dual-purpose machines, fleet numbers 3 and 4, entered the Gibson fleet when three of the Bedford machines were withdrawn to give Barlestone eleven vehicles, ie four Leylands and seven Bedfords. We endeavoured to sell the Bedfords but without success, so they were rather unusually sold at book value to LCT. We then discovered that some of the bus grant monies allocated to the Municipal sector had not been spent and this provided us with a worthwhile opportunity. We passed the Bedfords to a dealer, and took in part-exchange two more dual-purpose vehicles. One, as fleet number 10, was also unusual for LCT at this time for it possessed a Duple 53-seat body. This was in his stock colours so was put into LCT livery and entered service on 1st February 1981. The other vehicle was standing partly-finished at the Plaxton Scarborough factory and so was completed to our normal specification. As fleet number 11 it joined number 10 on 14th March 1981. Twenty-seven Dennis Dominator chassis were acquired during the year, 20 of these having leaf springs were fitted with the normal single-door East Lancashire 76-seat body as numbers 184, 240, 245, and 247 to 249 together with numbers 251 to 264 inclusive.

Five more with Marshall bodies became fleet numbers 226 to 230, and this left two vehicles (205 and 206) outstanding. Both had the standard East Lancashire body but both had air suspension, it having been decided to vary the original order. They came into stock in August 1980. The end result was that the last of

Only seven out of the entire Dominator fleet were not bodied by East Lancs, being provided by Marshalls. One of these, pictured below, was 227, which appear to have lost its last digit.

the Leyland PD3 buses with synchromesh gearboxes were eliminated from the stock, open rear platform buses being reduced to 20, all having semi-automatic transmission. LCT spent no less than £450,899 on new bus purchases during the year and received £339,699 by way of bus grant reimbursement. At a first glance the financial year-end situation did not look very good, as the difference between bus income and expenditure amounted to £135,199, and when other costs had been added the final result from operations amounted to £238,498. This, though, was offset by the usual testing station surplus of £69,537, profit on agency vehicle repair work and a Gibson management charge of £36,650, so the final net loss came out at £109,389 after making a very substantial contribution to the vehicle renewals fund of £480,000. Local Authority bus undertakings in membership of the association always sent out copies of their annual reports to their fellow members. I always perused these as they came in, and so was able to feel quite satisfied – well almost so – about our final results.

Next came 1st April 1981, which saw the start of the 1981 financial year and with it came the effects of some new Government legislation. The one that was going to affect us the most was the passing into law of the 1980 Transport Act. This was sponsored by Secretary of State Norman Fowler MP supported by his Junior Minister Kenneth Clarke MP. This piece of legislation turned things on their head. Prior to it becoming law, Road Service licensing had, ever since the passing of the 1930 Act, given established operator's considerable protection. If you were running a service and another operator came along and made

Municipal transport undertakings were united in their opposition to Norman Fowler's Transport Bill and mounted a concerted campaign against it. Across the country buses were painted in this striking overall livery of pink, white and blue. This bus belongs to the West Midlands PTE.

application to run over your route, either in whole or part, and take some of your passengers in the process, you objected to his application on the grounds of abstraction and unless you were very unlucky it was almost certain that your would-be competitor lost his case.

Nowhere was the end result more apparent that in the City of Leicester. When the 1930 Act was passed, Leicester City Transport had a sizeable and highly concentrated network of tramway lines, in the main of short length and all confined within the boundaries of the City. To protect these, the Area Stop Sign system was introduced. They were special castings, painted black, and were usually fixed about a quarter of a mile beyond each outer tramway terminus. From these points no bus belonging to any outside operator could pick up City-bound passengers, but could drop off those that had boarded the bus at a stop on the country side of the stop. The same applied to journeys working outwards. No in-city travel was permitted, but again passengers could be picked up who were travelling to points beyond the area stop so LCT had a complete monopoly of inside Leicester traffic. As the trams came to be abandoned and buses took over, the same restrictions continued to apply, the stop signs staying firmly in situ with only the one on Welford Road being eliminated thanks to that tortuous joint service agreement with Midland Red that covered the Wigston Magna and South Wigston services, numbers 63 and 62 respectively. Now the Fowler legislation pronounced that in future the Traffic Commissioners had to grant bus service applications, unless it was against the public interest to do so.

This was very ominous indeed, for this innovation and area stop signs did not seem compatible. It started with a County Travel attempt to be able to carry local traffic in the City along Welford Road. Needless to say LCT entered an objection, but this was only partly successful. County Travel were running their Fleckney to Leicester route at the time every two hours, so any passenger abstraction would be minimal, but now the company came forward with a much bolder proposal. It ran a second and unconnected service from Woodhouse Eaves to Loughborough, but now it made application to provide a through hourly-service from Fleckney through the City and on to Loughborough on an hourly basis, and of course carry local traffic from one end to the other. We went into some intense talks, the end result being that we deposited an application to work the proposed service on a joint basis from 4th March 1982.

If successful, then here would be another string to the Gibson bow. Pending a resolution, the Gibson fleet of four Leylands and seven Bedfords was augmented by a further two Leopard/Plaxton 53-seat dual-purpose vehicles, so the fleet strength was raised to 13 in anticipation of an additional requirement. These new Leopards became fleet numbers 1 and 2. Here was another pleasing factor as, thanks to the improvements made, Gibson vehicles were carrying an increased number of passengers in contrast to trends on the City services. Gibsons also possessed several excursion and tour licences which had seen little use in recent years. These were re-activated and 21 excursions were worked by Gibson vehicles during the year with financially beneficial results.

By this time the City offer to buy the local Midland Red routes had been reinforced to cover the more local ones that ran into Leicester from fairly near to

By 1982 Dennis Dominators were beginning to take over from the Metropolitans on front line service. Two examples are pictured in the city centre; numbers 61 and 62 being shown.

distant outer terminals. To this offer were added two material factors; LCT would provide any displaced Midland Red employee with a suitable job, and would also purchase any vehicles that were rendered surplus by such sales at fair valuation. We awaited a favourable answer to the proposals. In the meantime the County Council, which had legally a coordinating role to play, endeavoured to act as honest broker but with little success. Midland Red seemingly had its eyes fixed on the pot of gold that they apparently believed existed inside the boundaries set by the area stop signs, and also on the concessionary fares revenue enjoyed by LCT. The Traffic Commissioners were adamant that if concessions were offered to appropriate groups, then the cost of these had to be borne by the rate fund and not by other paying passengers.

At 31st March 1982 33,198 passes were in use. From 7th March the trip charge was raised from 2p to 5p, estimated to save the rate fund £300,000 in a full year, the City paying LCT £38.76 per pass issued by way of fare-make-up monies. Midland Red obviously felt that it should have a much bigger share of this very useful income than it had, for it only received its share of the pot in respect of the joint services and its Thurnby Lodge and Scraptoft operations.

Around this time I was asked if the City Council could not give LCT even more financial support, and my answer was that I did not want to see general subsidisation. If we were to be supported then I wanted the sums involved to be easily recognisable so that we would have the ongoing incentive to try to at least balance the books at the end of each financial year. The easy way out was for the Council to make up bus grant percentage payments as these continued to reduce from 50% to zero. This idea was accepted and introduced. The rate was now down to 30% and so the City made a contribution of £228,000 which brought LCT back to a full 50% offset. This injection of cash helped to fund the arrival of another 17 Dominator/East Lancs double-deck vehicles with some specification variations. Nine buses, fleet numbers 40 to 48, arrived with the standard three-speed Voith gear box, whilst numbers 49 to 52 had four-speed units which, thanks to the incorporated overdrive gearing, raised maximum vehicle speed from around 40 mph to 52 mph making them more acceptable when used on private hire operations. The last four, numbers 53 to 56, were fitted with Maxwell gearboxes as the first one was proving to be quite successful.

At this time East Lancs were experiencing some internal problems, so to help it was agreed that we would take an additional three double-deckers, again with three-speed Voith boxes, provided that LCT was not invoiced for them until the start of the next financial year. These eventually became numbers 57 to 59. All were fitted with air suspension. Additionally, bus number 45 had its Gardner engine replaced by a DAF unit, being returned to traffic on the 2nd April. There were now 224 buses in the LCT fleet with only seven open-platform buses in passenger service, plus one (Number 24) used for driver training. Twelve further PD3s and four Atlanteans were standing out of use prior to being sold and further 13 vehicles were on loan to the South Yorkshire PTE. But now came the bad news.

In August 1981 the Chief Executive and Regional Director of the NBC met with representatives of the City and LCT to answer the question that had been raised about a possible sale of appropriate routes and vehicles etc to LCT operation. The answer was a not very polite negative. Indeed, it went way beyond that word. Those of us present were told in no uncertain terms that the Midland Red that we knew of old would soon no longer exist. The Company was to be broken up into smaller units and one based on Leicester would by styled 'Midland Red East'. Co-ordination was required but LCT did not favour a Lancashire type of agreement and no wonder. Quite a number of the Company routes were non-viable and were being supported by the County Council. Co-ordinate and the City's solid revenue would find itself in company coffers whilst LCT would have to receive support from the County. But how long would such support be likely to continue, and if it did not, what then? Additionally, John Birks was moved to another post in NBC, which was not helpful.

Now, thanks to the passing of the 1980 Act, Leicester could be opened up at long last and the area stop sign system swept away, and so NBC now had a whole series of ideas in train that must bring this desired result into being. The spokesman was asked what these were, but no answer was forthcoming. This amounted to a declaration of war, and the meeting broke up, when goodwill all round was conspicuous by its complete absence. We eventually discovered just what was intended here after we had been given a copy of a report submitted by Midland Red East local management to the County Council dated 4th December 1981. It contained proposals to replace 25 local bus services with eight new cross-city services which would have no restrictions on the carriage of passengers except that the Company may impose minimum fares on certain selected afternoon peak departures to protect longer distance passengers. In addition, all restrictions, save for the type mentioned in the previous sentence, would be removed from 33 further services, effectively opening all Midland Red services to LCT passengers. The Company estimated that this would result in a net improvement of £300,000 per annum and a very small effect on LCT of about 3% of revenue. What a lot nonsense it was.

We were not prepared to see our traffic attacked in this way and so on 17th December a whole series of licence applications were deposited with the Traffic Commissioners. The County Council now tried to promote its co-ordinating role much more actively, but as battle was now joined it had little success and the talks it did manage to organise were desultory in the extreme. We prepared for a major Traffic Court battle by deciding that we needed the services of a skilled advocate and so our Chief Executive used his powers as a Solicitor to take steps to brief a

When this fine picture turned up I persuaded my Publisher that it was too good to leave out, so now you can have front and back, colour or black and white as you wish by comparison with page 127.

Barrister. We paid a visit on Monday 16th January 1982 to his London chambers which, to say the least, were just what one would have expected to find in the middle of the 1800s, whilst the electric wiring seemed to date from the same period. Our contact was very friendly but I wondered why we had approached him. He had, it was true, done Traffic Court work in the past, but that was some time ago. Now he was, shall we say, rusty and very much out of touch. Then he leaned back in his chair and proceeded to give us a blow-by-blow account of all the recent outstanding Traffic Court cases, naming the parties involved and the final results. Rusty indeed? Never!

We went over the local situation, he asked many questions, and then indicated he would accept the brief and made arrangements to come to Leicester and look over the territory very closely. This was going to be expensive, for as a QC he would have to be supported by a Junior, which meant paying two fees not one, but on the face of what we had heard that afternoon it was going to be money well spent. Now it was a question of waiting for the day when almost certainly our conflicting applications would come to be heard before the Traffic Commissioners. It was going to be serious, but fortunately some light relief now arose, as we shall see in the next chapter.

Prior to the passing of the 1980 Transport Act, LCT enjoyed a complete monopoly within Leicester. The new legislation encouraged the NBC to seek more traffic within the City, as described in the text. Midland Red's final double-deckers were Alexander-bodied Daimler Fleetlines as seen here. By the time of this photograph local operations had become branded as Midland Fox and the competitive situation I had anticipated had materialised.

# 9 – Time to Move On

I made a second trip to Krefeld, and one evening I was in the town's Park Hotel having a meal with some of the friends from Krefeld Verkehrs AG whose command of the English language was well nigh perfect. I was asked how I had come into transport, so I explained how as a young boy I had been interested in trams, and how by the age of around nine had decided that I wanted to have my name as General Manager on the side of a whole fleet of them.

The next question was "And have you succeeded in realising your ambition?" I had not and I had to tell the party that I never could as there was then only one working street tramway left in Britain, at Blackpool, where the current manager was a very old friend of mine but was a year or so younger than I was so I could expect to retire first, but in any event Leicester pay was higher than that offered by Blackpool Transport. We then passed on to talk of other things.

A few weeks later Mrs Cross brought in the morning's mail and in the pile was a letter from Krefeld saying that a gift was to be sent to me, which would consist of:-

One single deck overhauled bogie tramcar.
A matching single deck trailer.
A suitable generator.
The requisite overhead line fittings.
A kilometre of tramway track.

With it would come the instruction, 'Put your name on the side and have fun.'

I told the Members at the next Transport Committee of the letter and its contents when everyone was unanimous that the offers should be accepted. Consequently, on 15th September 1981 three very large articulated lorries arrived in Abbey Park Road and so after some 30 years the depot was once again housing railed vehicles.

We had hoped to have it running in due course hopefully in Abbey Park on a circular route linking the main gates with the riverside so Mr Edgeley Cox, the former Walsall General Manager and a noted electrical expert, was recruited to

Although the author never achieved his ambition to have his name on the side of a tram, he managed the next best thing which was to see it on the side of a fleet of motorbuses, appropriately here on a Dennis Dominator.

LEICESTER CITY TRANSPORT
ABBEY PARK ROAD   LEICESTER
G.G.HILDITCH  GENERAL MANAGER

act as adviser and we started to make tentative inquiries as to how much it might cost to have the track laid. But it was all in vain; the Government led then by Mrs Thatcher placed an embargo on unnecessary local authority spending and so I never did see a tram running in the manner proposed. I now have no knowledge as to what in the end happened to what was a magnificent gift and can only regret that we were never able to take Leicester people for a ride on tramway system mark two. I did though pay yet another visit to Krefeld where I named one of the undertakings brand new trams 'City of Leicester', a unit that also came to bear the City coat of arms.

So we came to the end of the year, a period that saw the departure of my Deputy Peter Goodridge after almost 44 years of service and the death of Albert Beeby. Albert had headed the testing station(s) ever since they opened and there was no doubt that his interest and enthusiasm had played a great part in the promotion of the business.

Smiles all round during the naming of a Krefeld tram 'City of Leicester'

At the 31st March 1982 there was a loss of £45,615 from LCT's bus operations. Add in bank charges etc and that loss rose to £89,705. This figure had to be offset by a £39,387 Gibsons' management charge, a testing station surplus of £74,431 and a profit of £22,463 from agency repair work, giving a net surplus of £46,576. This was realised after placing £829,000 into the vehicle renewals fund including the City Rate fund contribution of £228,000. Fares were raised from Sunday 7th March 1982 some thirteen months after the previous upward move.

Another unwanted expense occurred with effect from the 31st December 1981. Prior to that date a new bus was examined and if all was well then it received a Certificate of Original Fitness that was normally of seven years duration. During that period it had to be seen by a Department of Transport vehicle examiner at least once a year, but a good deal of flexibility was permitted. When the CoF expired overhaul took place, the bus was resubmitted and often a five year certificate would be issued. At the end of that time one for three years might be forthcoming and so the bus reached its 15th birthday which could well see the end of its life span. Perhaps though ordered replacements were late on delivery, so it was placed yet again before the Certifying Officer who might give it a final one of one or two years duration.

But now a full inspection had to be carried out each year when, if the vehicle passed, a certificate with a single year's life would be issued, and those inspections would normally have to be carried out at a DoT testing station. It was though permitted for an operator to have inspections carried out in his own premises, provided that a section was set aside for testing purposes and the equipment provided therein complied with DoT standards. We had met these requirements by installing a heavy duty brake tester, additional lifting jacks, headlamp beam setting and test meters, and a pit ventilation system. This was expensive, but it was not the end of the story for by way of a starter each annual test that took place, and we were providing all that was needed, attracted a charge of £29.00. This meant additional expenditure which with all the administration work involved was adding around £10,000 per annum to engineering costs.

So we came to 1st April 1982 and so entered what was to be (although I did not know it at the time) my last full financial year as General Manager of LCT. It was a year that passed very quickly with good times and those not so good. Despite the ongoing threats to LCT's financial well-being from Midland Red East that I will deal with later, high spots will be covered first starting with bus fleet changes.

Ten Dennis/East Lancs standard double-deckers had originally been ordered for delivery in the year, but three, numbers 56-58, had been built early by the Blackburn factory to help it over a short term order problem. Consequently, orders were placed for three more vehicles and these duly arrived as fleet numbers 67 to 69. We then called for an eleventh bus, which had a Dominator chassis, an East Lancs body, the usual Gardner engine and a Maxwell gearbox. This was placed on the Dennis stand at the 1982 International Motor Exhibition and entered the fleet later as number 70 when it displayed a slightly modified livery. An additional vehicle was also added to our order for two single-deck Duple-bodied Falcons (numbers 91 and 92). This was because Dennis wanted to hire one for fairly long term demonstration purposes and, of course, some bus grant was still on offer.

Five dual-purpose single-deckers had also been on order but here some alterations were made. Two of the new Leyland Tiger chassis with air suspension and Plaxton bodies arrived as numbers 16 and 17, whilst the three Dennis Dorchester chassis which were to have had similar bodies were now to be built with full luxury Plaxton coachwork and one was to have included in the specification a toilet, the use of which later was to quite intrigue me, as you will see. This left two other body orders to be considered. Duple's Blackpool factory was hard at work producing the three access buses and planning the routes to be operated was proceeding at Abbey Park Road as I had originally outlined, but their introduction was going to be rather special so it was decided to hold another formal handing over ceremony and a date was provisionally selected.

The last order to be catalogued here was totally unexpected. The Government suddenly announced with very short notice that the restrictions on capital expenditure would be relaxed provided that anything that might be wanted could be ordered, produced, completed and of course paid for by the financial year end. Here was a challenge. I went into negotiations with certain old friends, with the result that on 12th November 1982 orders were placed for five MCW Metrobus chassis and five low-height one-door Alexander double-deck bodies. These were delivered so as to go in service as fleet numbers 31 to 35 on 20th March 1983, which was surely a record for that period. The chassis cost £37,500 and the bodies £25,500 before a 20% grant deduction.

To achieve a quick delivery we had had to take low-height bodies that were then in production in Falkirk, but this meant they were very suitable for use on country routes where low trees abounded so three were finished in Gibson livery and allocated to Barlestone. That establishment was also given the four Leyland Leopard Willowbrook

The Spacecars looked very smart when finished in Gibson's livery. The legal lettering on the front reads GIBSON DIVISION. LEICESTER CITY TRANSPORT. When *we* put the lettering on it stayed put, unlike Willowbrooks as shown on the Spacecar on page 150!

Councillor Page, The Lord Mayor, becomes a conductor for the afternoon.

Spacecars so the last of the Bedfords could be sold out of stock, three being taken by new joint operator County Travel. Also taken out of stock were the last of the traditional type of front-engined double-decker bus namely the Leyland PD3s that had served Leicester so well, and with them went the last of the open platforms.

It was decided to mark the event in suitable ways, so on Saturday 2nd October 1982 the final survivors ran in service for the last time in the City. The Lord Mayor Councillor Page accepted the invitation to act as the conductor on one of them for the afternoon on the understanding that all the fares that he took would be given to his annual charity fund. He consequently bore, in addition to his chain of office, a cash bag, an ultimate machine and a supply of extra tickets. He and his passengers fully entered into the spirit of the event and every one seemed to enjoy themselves to the full.

Then on the Sunday we held an open day at Abbey Park Road. From early in the morning our staff and those of a good many of our suppliers worked to turn the garage and workshop into something resembling a market hall and in due course were more than ready to provide our visitors with demonstrations and explanations about what they were doing and why. Simultaneously, the catering department were setting up shop in the engineers offices that quickly took on the appearance of a cafeteria. We had planned to open at noon but by 11.00am a long queue had formed from the main gates along Abbey Park Road so we opened early when doubtlessly many of the scores of other visitors that followed the first ones had travelled to the event by bus after purchasing the special 70p adult or 45p child

THE
# LEYLAND TITAN PD3s
OF LEICESTER CITY TRANSPORT

Leicester CT withdrew its last Leyland PD3 on 2nd October 1982. To mark the event, the department produced a commemorative brochure, the cover of which is seen here. Yes, Mike Greenwood did get up at 4.20 am one morning to obtain this peaceful view at the clock tower.

tickets that gave freedom of travel all day on the LCT services plus a free ride on a PD3 operated City Tour. It was all highly successful, the biggest trouble coming at the end of the afternoon when we wanted to close up, but so many of our guests seemed very reluctant to leave. We were constantly asked when would we be repeating the occasion, but did not provide any specific answer. Open days had to be provided sparingly and so kept for what really were very special occasions.

If, however, the PD3s were going out, a PD2 came in. Some younger members of the staff who were very interested in buses generally told me that a Leicester PD2 still in Leicester livery remained apparently intact in a Barnsley scrapyard. This was too good an opportunity to miss, so we went into negotiation with the scrap man and he agreed to accept a redundant PD3 for his bus and so number 154 returned to Abbey Park Road. Delivered to LCT on 15th August 1950, 154 was based on chassis number 502647 and was fitted with a Leyland 56-seat body which was later increased to accommodate 61 seats. Placed in service on 1st December 1950, it formed part of the post-war tramway replacement fleet. It was last used in service on 27th March 1970 by which time it was painted in Leslie Smith's mainly cream livery which it still retained. It was then sold to a dealer who sold it on to a Scunthorpe area fruit farmer who used it very occasionally as a fruit picker transport vehicle until in September 1981 it was sold to the dealer.

I had it refurbished and put back into the livery it had originally carried when brand new, which later caused me some amusement. It was on display at some vintage event when I found myself stood by it in the company of two 'busologists' who had no idea who I was. One of them passed a sardonic comment on the character of a General Manager who had to have his name on both sides of the bus, but here they did not know that when new during the reign of Charles Stafford as General Manager, number 154 had borne his name and the rest of the legal lettering on both the near and off sides of the lower deck panelling. After overhaul and relicensing number 154 was able to carry fare paying passengers and so was put onto service when the owners of a new

Return of the prodigal. The 1950 all-Leyland PD2 154 stands inside our Abbey Park Road depot, restored to its original maroon and cream livery.

Two old friends stand ready to leave after giving good service to the City. Number 33, nearest the camera, is lettered recording the passing of the PD3s, and noting that Saturday 2nd October will be their last day in service. Below, number 82 saw further service in the area, now operating for Astil and Jordan Ltd and looking, dare I say it, very smart for an Independent operator. The passengers in the front seats have seen the photographer and are waving accordingly. Sometimes we see less charitable signs.

The last of the 1967 Leyland PD3As with East Lancs 74-seat bodies, No 16 (LJF 16F) has been preserved following withdrawal on 2nd October 1982. Here it attends a Leyland Celebration at the Crich Tramway Museum.

Beaumont Leys supermarket wanted to run some special trips from the City to mark the new stores opening day. I decided to have a drive and did one return trip being struck by the physical effort required thanks to no power steering, a manual gearbox, a heavy clutch and vacuum brakes that required a goodly amount of pedal pressure. The comparison between 154 and the Dominator that I drove next with its 'all mod con' features was really quite incredible.

Once again there were the inevitable wage and salary awards in the 1982/3 year. Clerical staffs had a 5.7% advance from the 1st July which meant £52,000 per annum additional cost, whilst on the 1st November traffic and engineering craftsmen had their weekly hours cut from 40 to 39 without loss of pay. These changes imposing load of £350,000 and £76,000 pa respectively. So nine months after the previous adjustment fares were raised as from 5th December 1982. Passenger recession continued with carryings falling from around 49 million to around 47½ but on the other hand private hire income rose from £233,000 to £304,300. We did not experience any extra in city competition from Midland Red East during the year and so were able to declare a small surplus of £120,904. This was after adding £778,633 to the bus renewals fund. In the year the bus grant payments dropped to 20% so the City upped its contribution to £409,000 so over £1m was added to the fund, but this was certainly needed as new bus prices continued to rise.

The first of the three Dennis Lances adapted for the Disabled Access Network is handed over to the Lord Mayor of Leicester at a ceremony in Abbey Park Road depot, following which all three buses were used to take invited guests on a tour of the routes.

There is though one administrative event to be recorded, as on 7th March 1982 the Gibson company was put into liquidation, so from the following day the unit became known as the Gibson Division of Leicester City Transport. Gibson's name and livery was retained for passenger identification purposes as Gibson vehicles had never carried local passengers along Hinckley Road and this situation continued in force.

But now I need to return to the saga of the proposed Access Services. Duple had promised a firm delivery date so it was decided that the handing over ceremony and a formal inauguration would take place on Friday 1st October 1982. I now began to be concerned that Duple production was not proceeding as expected, so just prior to the chosen day I told our Chief Engineer David Kent to take himself off to Blackpool and take with him a select band of brothers who could if the need arose help to complete at least one bus. I added that at least one working vehicle had to be at Abbey Park Road by 6.30am on the day and if it was not then there was no need to return at all. David and company duly left and came back with two buses around 6.37 am. Here was an historic event for they did not get away from the factory until midnight and on the way down the motorways they were fully engaged as bits of bus were being secured in situ.

Did I say two buses? Wrong! There was actually most of one and about half of the other, but David and his team had worked miracles and deserved a deal of praise for their efforts. I almost started to breathe again but the day was not yet started let alone over. The format was that Sir Peter Baldwin would inaugurate the service after the buses had been handed over by the manufacturers to the Lord Mayor, when Lord Crawshaw, a local dignitary who sadly was a wheelchair user, would be the first person to make use of the wheelchair lift.

Sir Peter arrived in Leicester by train. I met him at the station and we then went to Rutland Street where we were joined by Traffic Commissioner Mr Ken Peter, when I discovered that they had long been Department of Transport colleagues. We then went to the Lord Mayors Rooms to join the other guests who were welcomed by Chairman Councillor Henry Dunphy. Lunch was served, the Lord Mayor presiding and after the meal transport took the party to Abbey Park Road where the two vehicles stood on show, and after a quick look over them the formal proceedings began. The Chairman of Hestair Dennis Ltd, Mr David Hargreaves, and the Managing Director of Duple, Mr R West, handed the vehicles over to the Lord Mayor who in turn invited Sir Peter Baldwin KCB to inaugurate the Access Service. Sir Peter gave a short speech by way of response and then asked Lord Crawshaw if he would consent to being the first wheelchair occupant to make use of a lift. My Lord said he would be delighted so to do, and he was duly lifted from the garage concrete to the floor of the vehicle, when fortunately no one noticed that the head of our electrical shop Robin Woolley was holding the ends of a couple of cables together. Had he released his hold, Lord Crawshaw's upward journey would have come to a very sudden stop. After that piece of excitement a demonstration run followed when things became more relaxed and light refreshments were served. Like a certain Battle of Waterloo it was a very close run thing, and I breathed a whole series of sighs of relief as I bade our VIP'S farewell and thanked them for lending their presence to the event.

The public services began on 4th October using one bus crewed by driver George Crewe and conductor John Frankland, but it was soon obvious that even if the facility was not likely to even break even in the short term with fares of 50p or 35p depending on distance, then it certainly met a long desired need, as loadings slowly but surely built up, and with them came a quite unexpected development. A Mrs Cotterall of Evington realised that there was yet another need, and so she began to organise a 'pusher' service. A wheelchair passenger wanting to visit the City Centre could ring up and say when they would be arriving on one of our vehicles at the Clock Tower. Someone would be there to meet them and help them traverse the City Centre streets, which fortunately are almost level throughout the main shopping area and help with carrying any shopping. This led in turn to the organising of various social events, and I had the pleasure of attending some of them over the next few months. I also went on a journey. When the third bus was finally ready for delivery and our Duple suppliers had sworn that it was fully operational in every possible respect I went for it, took delivery and on the way back to Abbey Park Road made a diversion off the direct roads home.

This took me to a home for the disabled on the outskirts of Manchester and there I gave a demonstration of what it could do to a Mrs Joan Rigby who was an old family friend. Joan had had a sad life. Married shortly before the end of the war she lost her new husband on 8th April 1945 when, as a member of a Halifax bomber crew, he was killed when the plane was shot down over Germany. She remained a widow for some ten years before marrying for the second time, but then the disease multiple sclerosis struck and so Joan began to lose the use of her legs. Her husband also began to be ill with heart trouble and could not care for her, so she had to go to live in the home where she came to be deprived of all feeling below the waist. I would go and see her whenever I was in the area, and so I saw first hand just how difficult life was for her and the other similarly affected residents. I wished that there was something that could be done for them, and so Joan's plight was really the catalyst that led to the idea I put to Sir Peter at that Westminster Hall reception. I gave her a short run round the area, and then said I would see her again but alas her subsequent life was not to be of long duration, she passing away at the age of 63.

And so we reached 1st April 1984 when it was becoming rather obvious that the management of the Transport Department was losing its popularity; if, that is, it had ever had any. The first significant sign was when the ruling Labour Group failed to agree internally that my long term Chairman Councillor Henry Dunphy should be reappointed to that position. Henry had held the post for several years and was very much a transport man. When I first met him as a Committee Member back in 1975 he had been employed by British Rail, but prior to that he had worked for LCT as a bus driver. Consequently, he knew the undertaking as it were from the bottom, but although a committed Labour party supporter, I was never in any doubt that if an occasion arose when the political need and a transport need were incompatible the transport part of the argument would win. His place was taken by a gentleman whose local government career was of short duration and sadly we were not together long enough to forge the sort of relationship that was desirable, which was a pity.

Then, on the afternoon of Sunday 18th March I was sat in the lounge at home toasting myself before the fire when the phone rang. I answered it to take a call from the Rutland Street shift charge inspector, who told me he had just had a call from police headquarters. Could we send ten coaches with drivers to the Enderby Control Centre for 10.00 pm that night, but we should be aware that they might be away on hire for quite a time. When asked could he find ten drivers the answer was in the positive, so I told him to tell the police we could and would and I would liaise with the engineering department and have the vehicles prepared. I must confess that pound signs came into my eyes. A ten vehicle long term hire must be very lucrative and if you could not trust the police to meet the resulting bill who could you trust?

I went down to Abbey Park Road about nine o clock to find men and machines all ready for the off and about a half hour later they drove off into the night. From time to time one would re-appear for fuelling etc, and it did seem that the drivers were quite enjoying their unusual form of outing but then down came the shutters. I was told the hire had to cease as local thought was intent on supporting the miners in their current struggle. I could not help thinking that this was putting the cart before the horse as nearly all the miners in Leicestershire and Nottinghamshire were working, being incensed that they had been instructed to down tools instead of being allowed a free vote on the issues. It seemed that our coaches were taking officers to pits that were threatened with the arrival of flying pickets intent on stopping those working going to work so who was supporting who? Well, I am not a politician so when the stop was confirmed at the next transport committee that was then accepted policy and that is what General Managers have to follow. We then had a spot of union trouble. Our long serving Union Secretary had to retire on health grounds and the way in which a subsequent settlement after some acrimonious meetings was reached did leave me wondering.

Prior to this, Thursday 26th May 1983 had seen the launch of a pretty ambitious project. The origin lay in a Burnley and Pendle Transport initiative when that operator began a daily service from Burnley to London. This ran south in the morning returning from London in the late afternoon but the carriage of intermediate journey passengers was not possible as there were no suitable picking up or setting down points en route. I was told of this piece of enterprise by Roy Marshall, the then Burnley and Pendle General Manager, and suggested his vehicles made a diversion taking in Leicester and offering travel to and from Lancashire at the very least. So he went off to think the idea over. This gelled and then Maidstone Transport joined in.

We had noted that the Reading and Southend undertakings had started running express buses into London and had then linked the two operations together to give a through service from one town to the other. We could do likewise and so the City Flyer service took off. This ran from Blackpool to Dover travelling via Blackburn, Accrington, Burnley, Todmorden, Sowerby Bridge, Halifax, Sheffield, Leicester, London, Maidstone and Folkestone. In London the vehicles used the Gloucester Road coach station, but also had a stop on the Embankment. Each of the three partners allocated vehicles to the service; Maidstone drivers worked in the main from Dover to London, Leicester men covered the Burnley to

Plaxton-bodied Leyland Tiger coach 17 stands in Sheffield's Pond Street bus station on a southbound journey on the City Flyer. The Hyde Park flats in the background have long since been demolished. Below, at the other end of the route, a Burnley and Pendle coach arrives in Dover on an equally wet day.

London part, and Burnley staff were to be seen between Blackpool and Leicester, but the vehicles of the three parties ran through to either of the outer terminals.

From the LCT point of view the new Dennis Dorchesters, with their coach bodies, were ideal for the route, and had an additional item contained in the specification which included those standard components the Gardner 6LXB engine in horizontal form, a Voith four speed gearbox with retarder, power steering and air suspension. The extra unit was a two speed rear axle. In built up areas this gave a better performance if kept in the lower speed higher gear ratio but once the motorway was gained the high speed low ratio gearing could be brought into use thus promoting a useful higher top speed and fuel economy.

A Leicester bus went into the circuit at Rutland Street which was used as our city calling point. It would be taken and parked in the yard to await the arrival of the southbound vehicle. The duty controller would oft times ask over the radio for anyone who sighted the Flyer approaching the City to call in, and on receipt of the news the controller alerted the canteen staff who then brewed the tea and made sure refreshments were laid out for the delectation of our passengers. Once the vehicle was in the yard and the travellers had entered the building all the passengers items were carefully transferred to the new coach and placed in identical locations.

Consequently, as the interior finishes were all to the same pattern, moquette etc, few realised that they were not leaving on the same vehicle that had carried them into Leicester. That vehicle then ran through to Dover, then began its run north being refuelled in Maidstone. It passed through London to reach Leicester but did not stop, continuing to Blackpool to be serviced either at the Lytham St. Annes depot or in Burnley before continuing south to Rutland Street where it came off service and its replacement went on, when in its turn the coach with the toilet would be allocated to the schedule.

I travelled on the service as regularly as possible always talking to the passengers and seeking their views on the operation and here came the surprise. Quite often a driver would be asked by a passenger would he please call at a service area so the passenger could use a toilet, but when the toilet equipped coach was involved this did not happen, and it was not because the on board facilities were well used but quite the contrary. I came to the conclusion that just the thought that there was one always to hand gave our more elderly customers a feeling of confidence, and now at the perhaps over ripe age of 87 I am fully aware of what can come with a multitude of years.

Normally there were long stretches when no stop was made. So after leaving Sheffield and joining the M1 the next stop was Rutland Street and after leaving Leicester it was non stop down the M1 to Willesden Green on the edge of London. It was a long route, both in terms of time and distance. For example, the 12.30am departure from Dover arrived at Gloucester Road at 3.00am and departed 15minutes later. It then reached Rutland Street at 6.15am where there was another 15 minute halt. The Sheffield departure was timed at 7.55am and Burnley was reached at 9.45am, where there was a 30 minute halt before the coach left for Blackpool to arrive at the Rigby Road Coach Station for 11.30am. At Burnley connections were made with the Lonsdale Coach Services route to

Lancaster, Morecambe and Heysham. Other winter timetable departures from Dover left at 5.30am and 2.30pm. There was also a 'short' working linking Maidstone and Blackpool. One big difficulty, if not the biggest, was how to ensure the service was given adequate publicity, so the vehicles were fitted with quite distinctive displays and we did what we could through local channels, but word of mouth and passenger satisfaction must play its part. This was soon apparent in good measure and few complaints were received. The through fare from Dover to Blackpool was £40.00 period return or £26.50 single. There was no need to pre book as tickets were sold on the coaches, but a number of booking agents were recruited. As was to be expected loadings were initially quite light but did build up, it being agreed that the operation would be continued for a trial period of 18 months. I realised that having all the coaches toilet-fitted could be a big selling point so three more Dorchester/Plaxton vehicles were ordered to be so fitted, and I tried to persuade our partners to follow suit. The City Flyer was labelled as route number 100.

At last the Traffic Commissioner announced that four days would be set aside in May 1984 when he would hear the competing applications deposited by Midland Red East and LCT, so our Barrister and his Junior arrived in Leicester and prepared themselves for the fray. By the time of their arrival things had moved on and so a strategic review was called for. So at this point in the narrative let us describe what had occurred. By April 1982, two sets of competing applications had been produced by the operators and the County Council was endeavouring to come to some decisions as to which, if any, should be endorsed by virtue of its role as co-ordinating authority. The County Council then asked both operators to withdraw these applications and to consider further the possibility of a wider co-ordination scheme being introduced.

A number of talks then took place but no solution was forthcoming. The Company was anxious to maintain 'scale', wanting to keep its present mileage and vehicular requirements whilst to give LCT adequate income some considerable adjustments would have been necessary. Eventually, at a meeting held in the Midland Red (East) offices in August 1982, the local manager said that in his view co-ordination would obviously offer little benefit to LCT, a remark which in view of what had gone before aroused my suspicions. Subsequently, a new pattern emerged. In the interests of apparent economy, the Company was formulating a set of new route proposals which varied the original Company ambition to concentrate as many local services as possible on St. Margaret's Bus Station in the interests of improved control. Instead services were to be taken out of the Bus Station, put on to street stands where in many instances they would be competing with LCT workings, and so intensify the competitive aspect a whole series of cross-city links were proposed.

In the meantime, the County Council, in an endeavour to arrive at some acceptable settlement, had held a tripartite meeting at County Hall on 25th June 1982. At the end of this meeting a paper was produced with the title 'Bus Services in Central Leicestershire' which attempted to set out the current position of the two operators, but with a target date of 1st July 1983 for the removal of restrictions on loading and protective fares.

Two examples of Leicester's coach fleet are shown here. Above is number 15, a Leyland Leopard with Willowbrook Spacecar body which would later be transferred to the Gibson fleet, while below is 16, one of the pair of Plaxton Supreme Express-bodied Leyland Tigers which were used on the City Flyer service, now painted in the new red and grey post 1984 livery. Sharp - eyed readers will see that Willowbrook's s i g n w r i t i n g department leaves much to be desired as letters have dropped off – sadly this was not all that was below par as the narrative explained earlier.

Doubtless the Midland Red Officers were encouraged in their endeavours by the contents. By 31st March we had heard that some of the original proposals had been modified by the Company but no precise details had come to hand. We sought to obtain these via the County Council.

At this point we must return to strategic options. LCT seemed to have two. The first was to mount the competitive applications already mentioned, and here it is pertinent to mention that these were of a limited nature being based primarily on the number of vehicles that could be found from existing resources, plus the retention of those that would normally be taken out of stock when new ones came to hand. It was appreciated that some extra manpower would have to be recruited, and those factors plus the extra mileage involved would result in additional expenditure being incurred.

The second alternative was to do nothing, and let the status quo continue. This seemingly negative response to forthcoming events appeared to offer three advantages; firstly no additional operating costs would be involved. secondly it would be possible to quite accurately assess just what Midland Red (East) competition was costing, and thirdly the County Council when asked to provide LCT with some solid financial support would not be in a position to challenge the basis upon which claim was being made. In the event at the very last minute the Authority decided to adopt this latter policy much to the chagrin of our Barrister who had based his intended case on ensuring that LCT gained its competitive applications. He was now left with the task of defending the indefensible. He certainly did his very best but the outcome was never in doubt. Midland Red (East), or Midland Fox as it became, gained all it had sought whilst LCT was to continue operationally as of yore.

When the decisions of the Traffic Commissioner came to hand on Wednesday 16th May, I did some deep thinking, and it was all too obvious that life was never going to be the same again. LCT had been well run in the past and very successful, but initially at least it would become dependant on the County Council for support and its freedom of action could well come to be somewhat limited, but this was not the only problem looming large on the horizon. Nicholas Ridley's 'White Paper with Green Edges' was now in the process of being transformed into law, the enabling Bill being published on Thursday 12th July, and with it would come two interesting factors.

The idea of seeking competitive applications was to give LCT some bargaining power. If war had broken out on the streets and both operators were losing money the County Council was not likely to offer any supper to either, so it would be a case of saying you are hurting us, but we are hurting you, so let's get together and try to come up with some satisfactory solutions. But this new legislation was going to prevent operators from agreeing deals as competition was going to be the name of the game.

The other factor was intriguing. The National Bus Empire was to be broken up and sold off, so presumably had Leicester City Council been so minded it could have dusted off its earlier wish to acquire all the Midland Red services in the City and so make a bid to purchase the later Midland Fox concern subsequently acquired by Drawlane. It could then have sold off the parts it did not want running in the outer areas. True, its City routes could become subject to the competition element mentioned above, but it would have been in a virtually unassailable position. No such proposal was ever mooted, but if it had been what might the attitudes of the Department of Transport and the County Council to it have been? That we will never know.

At the end of the day I came to the conclusion that my only option was to sit tight, to do the best of my ability all that I had to, and take early retirement when I reached the age of sixty, my birthday not being all that far away. But I was lucky here as I was offered early retirement with an enhanced pension so I readily accepted the offer and made ready to depart from Leicester for our Torbay holiday home at the earliest convenient date, filing my copy of the Ridley White Paper for which I was going to have no further use. Or so I thought. Just how wrong can one be? Unfortunately, this early development prevented me from following up a very promising line of enquiry.

Contemporary thought suggested that if one saved a ton of weight from a bus you would save around a mile per gallon of fuel usage. I have already described the Maxwell gearbox that was lighter than the Voith and not having torque converter offered a better fuel economy thanks to the fitting of a more economical fluid flywheel.

I had been in discussion with Paul Gardner of the Gardner Engine family, only the company was now part of the Hawker Siddeley Group. Paul had been developing a five-cylinder engine, the 5LXCT, which, on the test bed, had surprised Paul and his colleagues by the strength of its performance. Weighing 758kg the 8.7-litre 5LXCT produced 170bhp at 1,850rpm. The compression ratio was 15 to 1. Compare these statistics to those of the 6LXCT which weighed 908kg, was of 10.45-litres capacity and produced 230bhp at 1,900rpm. As this engine was normally de-rated to give 160bhp for ordinary bus use and with a definite weight saving of 150kg or some 640lbs, the apparent advantages of going for five cylinders is immediately obvious.

It was agreed that one of the six or so prototypes would be delivered to Leicester, coupled to a Maxwell gearbox, put into a Dominator, and then run on extensive trials when we expected to have saved that ton, and also gained some useful space in the engine compartment. The engine was delivered and reputedly installed, but legend has it that it perhaps made just two trial runs when deemed not fit for purpose. It was removed, after which its fate appeared to be shrouded in mystery. Retired LCT engineering staff involved at the time, say it was returned to Patricroft but Paul Gardner is adamant that it never came back to the factory, and so I would really like to know just what did happen to it. Certainly neither that engine nor the Maxwell boxes were around in 1990 as I was able to discover for myself.

My remaining days passed quickly, and then when I was getting close to my departure date the unexpected happened. The phone rang and the receptionist asked would I take a call from a lady from the Department of Transport? I answered in the affirmative, and so my caller came on the line to ask if a Mr Brown could come and see me and mentioned a possible date. I indicated that I was not then available so I suggested a couple of alternatives, but who was Mr Brown? I had never heard of him but of course did not say so. It appeared that Mr Brown, later Sir Patrick Brown, was the Under Secretary in charge of the Civil Service team that was involved in doing what the Civil Service had to do, to turn the Governments' White Papers into law. I went on to suggest that she should ask Mr Brown which alternative he preferred, and then ring me back, and also tell me which train he would be taking from London when I would meet him at the station. She duly did, so I told her that my car, a dark blue Jaguar, would be parked in the station forecourt and that I would be leaning on the radiator so there should be no identification problems.

So it came to pass on Friday 10th August that I managed to attain pole position right in line with the exit from the booking office, so when a stranger carrying a brief case stamped OHMS appeared I realised that here was my expected visitor. We met, shook hands and took our seats in the car, for the short journey to Abbey Park Road where over coffee our conversations began. He said that it had been suggested to him that he should have a talk with me, although I was not told who made the suggestion. He assumed that I had read the Ridley White Paper so what did I think about the contents. I replied that I was too old a hand to be caught out by such a question. I was working for a Labour controlled Local Authority which was very well aware of the document and its contents, and the members were much opposed to the implied intentions. We chatted on, moving to Rutland Street for lunch and then came the big surprise.

It had emerged in our talks that my stay in LCT was not going to be of a very long duration; about one week in actual fact. So I was asked what I was going to do in my retirement. At this time I had no plans in mind for the future and said so. Mr Brown, as he then was, being the Permanent Secretary in the Department of Transport, said that the Department felt it needed to engage the services of a professional transport adviser to help it in its work. He then asked if I would I be interested in joining the Marsham Street team on a temporary two day a week basis?

I had a quick think. We were going to take up full time residence in our Torbay holiday home, but there was a very good train service from Newton Abbot to London. So why not? I thanked him for the offer and said that I would be delighted to accept.

Thus did I arrive at my very last day as General Manager of Leicester City Transport, namely Wednesday 22nd August 1984. I went to the office as usual that morning and did what I had to do, and quietly put into my bag those items of property that belonged to me. Then I went to Rutland Street to receive my last luncheon visitor, this being Traffic Commissioner Mr Ken Peter who was both surprised and pleased to hear of my impending DoT appointment, as in earlier days Patrick Brown had worked there with him. During our ensuing conversations he asked me why the LCT counter applications had been withdrawn but I had to tell him that I simply did not know. The reason, and there must have been one, was

Perhaps the least attractive of the Atlanteans delivered to Leicester were those fitted with Metro-Cammell bodywork. Number 187 is seen here showing one of the shortcomings of this livery and reinforcing the importance of regular washing of the fleet.

Looking at these pictures of vehicles which came from one or another of the Leyland Group factories put me in mind of a certain meeting with Mr Trevor Webster at Leyland Headquarters when he informed me that there would be no more Fleetlines – and his rather smug question in response to my understandable annoyance – well where else are you going to go for an alternative? Perhaps if Mr Webster had been able to see into the future he would have known that actually he would hold the answer and we would be able to resume our friendship! The buses shown are both from an order for 20 Atlanteans, delivered in 1969/70, ten bodied by Eastern Coach Works (above) and the remainder by Park Royal (below). Both bodybuilders, along with Charles Roe in Leeds, were part of the so-called Leyland Empire at that time. It was then busy engineering its own downfall, although it couldn't see it.

One of the first fleets to take examples of the Metro-Scania single-deckers was Leicester and the commonality of design with the double-deckers was instantly obvious, not least in the asymmetrical windscreen. Number 224 is seen above, and 297 below.

never explained to me. Incidentally, when I was writing this part of the manuscript I rang my old Chairman Henry Dunphy, to ask if over the years since he had discovered the reason. His reply was that he had not and was as much in the dark as I was. It is all water under the bridge now and there is no point in speculating what might have been but Mr Peter made his views very plain. If the Fowler Act was going to let Midland Red East run over our routes then we had the right to run over theirs, and it had been his intention to grant every one of our applications. It is a pity he never had the chance so to do. Still I would be leaving in around three hours so the problem was no longer mine, it would be up to the new management in whatever form it was to take, to cope with the resulting and on going effects.

As I was leaving I did not come to be much involved with some other Council developments. Obviously thinking that the electorate should be made fully aware of all the good things that the Council was doing on its behalf, a Public Relations Department was brought into being with, of course, the requisite staff. Its initial impact on LCT was minimal but somewhat frustrating. If an organiser had written in earlier asking if it would be possible for a party to be shown over the depot and workshops the letter would be passed to the Chief Engineer, when either he or his assistant would liaise with the organiser, agree a suitable date and time for the visit, and when it took place they would ensure that sufficient guides were on hand to escort the visitors around the premises. Now such requests had to be passed to the Publicity Department which then commenced a two way liaison with LCT and the organiser to come in due course to agreeing some suitable arrangement when a Publicity representative had to be present.

The next item of corporate thought was more monumental. All Council vehicles were to display a standard livery and the name of each departmental Chief Officer was no longer to be applied to the panelling, which in LCT terms meant that the legal wording would be simply 'Leicester City Transport Abbey Park Road Leicester'. The Leslie Smith livery of cream with maroon bands would disappear as the vehicles came to be repainted and a very different red and grey colour scheme would be substituted. Here though it was shades of Frank Lincoln, namely a new livery coming along with a new management only on this occasion the inspiration did not come from inside the walls of Abbey Park Road. As it transpired no vehicle was repainted before I left office, the new style first appearing on the streets on 7th October 1984.

Leaving as I did at the end of August, I did not have time to produce an annual report for the year ending the 31st March 1984, but in due course a shortened form did appear over the signature of the then Chairman of the Transport Committee, and not the Director of Transport as my successor was entitled. This stated that the full effect of Midland Red East competition had still to be felt (the area stop sign system having been abolished from the 1st July 1984) but indicated that with a fares increase in December 1983 of 10% a surplus of £142,265 was made after taking into account the payment of £330,000 from the council. In the 1984/85 report that was also signed by the Chairman it was said that competition had cost the undertaking a minimum of £140,000 in the first nine months after the abolition of the area stop sign system but the words 'In reality it was probably far higher' were added later.

Once the Dennis Dominator, the development of which had involved me in some small way, was available it became Leicester's standard double-decker. Two examples are seen, a Marshall-bodied specimen above with the lower vehicle, from East Lancashire Coachbuilders, showing the later Leicester City Bus livery, though after my departure.

By now the Ridley Transport Bill was pursuing its way through Parliament and it was becoming more and more obvious as it did so that the changes wrought by 31st March 1985 were only a prelude to more changes which would bring unforeseen consequences in their train. I do not propose to comment in detail on the contents of these annual reports as it is not my place to do so, but I did read them carefully when an interesting item stuck my eye. The City Flyer service was withdrawn at the end of October 1984, the receipts for the express service being shown as £53,753 for the year to 31st March 1984. However the same figure for the following part year only was stated as £91,765. Could it be that traffic had increased significantly or was there some other explanation? For example was the undertaking now running some new ventures locally that came under the express services heading?

This is a question I cannot, of course, answer, but if the original status quo had been maintained in Leicester could it have been a permanent feature? It was, at the very least a bold innovation. As it was the three Dennis Dorchester coaches new in my day were exchanged for a like number of Dominators equipped with Alexander style bodies, whilst the three on order at the date of my departure found new homes with another Municipal operator. Thus did Abbey Park Road and I part company, for what I was certain would be finality, but as Volume Four of "Steel Wheels and Rubber Tyres" will show my assumption was very, very wrong.

When I left Leicester I thought I would have more time for model making. Wrong again!

**FACING PAGE**

Leicester is quite well represented at rallies and other events where restored buses gather for the enjoyment of enthusiasts and others who just remember riding on them to work or perhaps to the cinema. The oldest survivor is this splendid three-axle AEC Renown dating from 1939 with its distinctive Northern Counties body. The Leyland bodied Leyland Titan PD2 has to be one of the all-time classic designs whilst the later Titan PD3s show the difference a change in livery can make. The later AEC Renown, with its low height design, contrasts with the Metropolitan double-decker.

Leicester vehicles from the ranks of the many preserved buses and coaches continue to fly the flag at various rallies up and down the country, proudly bearing the name Hilditch as the General Manager. Here a Metro Scania single-decker poses in bright sunshine at Dunsfold in Surrey in April 2011 whilst below, on a more sombre day, newly restored Dominator number 50 is seen at Long Marston when the Showbus event was held there in September 2014.